MARDYAN

What Was Meant
FOR MY BAD...

Made Me Better

All scriptures taken from the King James Version of the Bible

The opinions expressed in this manuscript are solely the opinions of the author and do not represent the opinions or thoughts of the publisher. The author has represented and warranted full ownership and/or legal right to publish all the materials in this book.

What Was Meant for My Bad...
Made Me Better
All Rights Reserved.
Copyright © 2015 Mardyam Hardrick
v2.0

Cover Photo © 2015 thinkstockphotos.com. All rights reserved - used with permission.

This book may not be reproduced, transmitted, or stored in whole or in part by any means, including graphic, electronic, or mechanical without the express written consent of the publisher except in the case of brief quotations embodied in critical articles and reviews.

Outskirts Press, Inc.
http://www.outskirtspress.com

ISBN: 978-1-4787-5071-0

Outskirts Press and the "OP" logo are trademarks belonging to Outskirts Press, Inc.

PRINTED IN THE UNITED STATES OF AMERICA

MARDYAM HARDRICK
WHAT WAS MEANT FOR MY BAD… MADE ME BETTER!

The story of how consistent occurrences of physical, mental and emotional child abuse (that should have destroyed me), shaped me into the dynamic woman that I am today. Through the constant hail of attacks by family members (and others), my demise surely should have been certain. But God….!

AUTOBIOGRAPHY-

I dedicate this book to the people who knew me during my adolescence and recognized my intellectual abilities then; but was not able to recognize the terror that plagued and threatened those abilities. And now some might feel the need to state their opinion on the outcome of me as an adult. They've been known to say, "Mardyam should be doing more than what she's doing. She should be the head of some multi-billion dollar corporation or something." I do appreciate the lesson lived and learned where the world has a lot to say…and yet does little… but God does it all. I want to share this testimony of some of what He brought me through and why I live today.

I extend a special dedication and thanks to my fourth grade teacher, Mrs. Wilson, from Springdale Memphis Magnet School.

And finally, I dedicate this book to all the people "still in the struggle".

Contents

Foreword i
Introduction 1
How It All Got Started 5
The Transfer Of The Demon 16
The Move From The Hood 20
Another Bad Home 27
Mo Money (Mo Problems) 41
Who's Yo Daddy 52
The Birth Of Lujanette 54
Leaving Memphis 63
Doing Me 69
Meeting Daddy Samuel 79
Right Choice Wrong Time 82
The First Marriage 86
Returning To Memphis 94
Another Marriage 97
The Final Straw 106
Restoration 111

Foreword

I AM WRITING this book to share some of the experiences I've had along my life's journey. My testimonies will help persuade you in believing that bad things in your life can indeed be used to launch you into a rich and fulfilling place. I want to encourage you not to live as if circumstances have you defeated; but rather as you have the victory over those occurrences we deem unfortunate. It is of course duly noted that life does have its' own unique DNA and heartbeat for each of us. Our experiences through life does help shape who we become. My thought is that we should be the greatest at whomever we are and learn to appreciate the person we've become.

Initially, I was excited about writing this book, of course, but that was about ten years ago. Today, I sit and ponder, "Do I really want to expose myself to the world, especially now when I have four children and two grandchildren who might someday pick this up and read it." Then as I continued to ponder, I realize that my issues are a lot of people's issues and should be shared.

I wonder if the people who know me now will better understand how I turned out to be who I am. Will they believe that I once hated myself and was suicidal (especially since I show so much love for myself today, even exposing a little bit of arrogance)? Well, will they believe that I lived in a state of chronic depression for years, but now I am able to spread genuine joy everywhere I go? (People often tell me that I should have been a comedian because I keep them laughing. (Maybe after this book!)) When they learn that I was a victim of child abuse, molestation and rape, will they wonder how I was able to deal with it all? What will they think about my once promiscuous lifestyle, sleeping with whomever, even indulging in bisexual activities. I do say once promiscuous because although I am still a little flirty today, I no longer indulge in sexual activities loosely.

Perhaps it just may be that my life, all or in part, bear resemblance to the lives of many who read this.

I hope that after you read about my life experiences that you will consider parts you can relate to and then where there is guilt let it be removed. If there is still anger from what someone has done to you, turn that anger into passion to help the next person make it through what you've come through. If there is pain, know that in time it will be healed. If you are still here then learn to laugh, laugh, laugh, because that thing (whatever it was), didn't kill you. It wasn't great enough to do so. That means you actually have power over it. That's why one must laugh. Embrace yourself with your own love. Work on perfecting the you that you have become.

So now walk with me as I share my testimony!

Introduction

WHEN MAMA GOT pregnant this time around, Paul was already incarcerated. Already a victim of domestic violence, she had to know that it would be pretty much suicidal to mess around on Paul, besides bring another man around his son, especially while he was serving time in the Penn. But I guess the pull to fill the empty void that was inside her soul due to Paul's absence was stronger than the worry of 'what if' I get caught cheating. I guess she figured that there could no harm come from having a friend around to help past the time, just as long as things didn't get out of hand of course. As long as there would be no evidence left behind that someone else had been there then that old cliché 'what you don't know won't hurt you' would stand.

Now I hear that Samuel, the gentleman that was helping mama past the time while waiting on Paul, was a very nice man. He was mild mannered and very respectful to women, I guess except to the one woman that he was actually married to who just happened not to be my mother. Mama tells me that she has never heard him even raise his voice. Whenever he was around peace dominated the atmosphere, something so different than when Paul was there; so, needless to say, mama felt safe in his presence.

But one day something terrible happened. Things did get out of hand. Something came over Samuel and he began to lose control of his typically very 'under control' self. It took my mama right by surprise she tells me today as we casually chat. All of a sudden, he forced her to the floor leaving her virtually no time to react. Her pleas of "No, no! Please don't!" fell on deaf ears as he wrestled her to the point of exhaustion and took what he wanted.

Thus I was conceived! And I would surely be plenty of evidence left behind that someone else had been there. No, I wasn't made out of the love that two people shared between each other, but out of an adulterous situation gone horribly wrong (or maybe gone just right depending on whose point of view you're looking from). In essence, I Am the result of my daddy date raping my mother.

Mother of course panicked. With Paul getting out soon and Samuel being married she knew that she had to do something. She was caught between a rock and a hard place. This situation was nothing but bad for her and she felt that there was absolutely no way that she could keep this child. Besides that, she was still living at home with her own mother and already had brought one baby in the house, Paul's son Nathaniel. She did not want to bring in another one to shelter under her mother's roof. What were her choices though? She had no money for the abortion she wanted to have. What was she going to do? Desperation finally set in and she decided to poison her own self just to kill me. She swallowed some kind of toxic pills and drank turpentine; a colorless, flammable strong smelling oil, which together was supposed to rid the body of any foreign objects. To her I was a foreign object, but doesn't she know that a baby in the uterus is not foreign; that the sole purpose of the uterus is to hawse and nurture a baby. Well, as you might notice though, that didn't work. I was already made stronger than toxic pills and turpentine. At that now I can laugh.

I was born March 28, 1970 in Memphis, Tennessee to Annette Hardrick. Paul Johnson would serve as my daddy. I was the second of their three children and the only girl that would be born into this small family. Although I got here by what we would classify as an unfortunate mishap, I am here because destiny said that I should live any way and not die. If you are here then clearly destiny has said the same thing concerning you. Since death and destruction were not allowed to capture me in the womb however, they did silently wait for me to make my entry into their cruel world and began to launch their attacks against my young life.

Since my mother had to bring me forth anyway, she at least hoped that I would be a boy. She had pre-maturely purchased boy clothes for me and even had a boy's name picked out and ready. She and her sister sometimes would bicker about my sex. "I don't know why you are buying those boy clothes for", aunt Freda would say. "This is going to be a girl." Mama just wasn't having that. She hadn't taken one minute to plan life for me as a girl and had not one ounce of desire to have a daughter share her life, so imagine her astonishment when the doctor announced, "it's a healthy baby… girl". "Did that doctor say that I had a girl? Well I'll be damned!"

My name for the first three days of my life was simply Girl, Hardrick. It wasn't until Annette was about to be discharged from the hospital that the nurse beckoned for her to name me, "Mrs. Hardrick, we've got to get this girl named before you get out of here." But my mother had nothing! That's when another lady who was on the labor and delivery ward decided to help and gave me my name, Marti. Yet determined to have some part of her 'boy', my mother selected Andre` as my middle name. I went from Girl Hardrick to Marti Andre` Hardrick which is the official name that's documented on my birth certificate but surely will not be the name documented on my death certificate.

Even after mama got me home she was still so hung up on having what she wanted that she dressed me like a little boy. Her detachment to the girl me was so apparent that Aunt Freda asked her for custody of me to rear as one of her own. Mama had too much pride to give me away though. In other words, she didn't really want me but didn't want anyone else to have me either. Have you ever heard that saying before? You probably associate it to intimate relationships between man and woman all the time. It is all a form of pride and anybody can have it concerning anything. You see, to give me away would be admitting that she was not quite capable of being a suitable mother for me. When a person knows that they don't possess what's needed for the positive nurture and growth of another person but they pretend that they do for the sake of their own reputation, they are filled with pride. Such prideful people will not accept the smallest amount of help from an outside source especially if they think the source has been made aware that they lack certain capabilities. So then the innocent one is left to suffer. In this case me; and suffer I did.

Listening to her share the stories over and over about how she did not want a girl fused into my young soul a sense of rejection that became the foundation for the enemy to build a fortress upon. That was the first of many weapons that would be formed against me (some were formed by others and some I formed myself) and the first of many that in the end would be destroyed.

-1-

How It All Got Started

GROWING UP IN the 'hood' where sex demons dwelt among family members and where domestic violence ruled the household would inevitably have devastating effects on my life. The hood for the entire Hardrick family was located right there off of Springdale Street in the North Memphis part of town. We could either be found on Springdale and Brown, Springdale and Howell, Springdale and Etheridge, just Springdale and something.

My memory takes me back to when we lived on Springdale and Brown in a widespread apartment complex known as the Yellow and Whites. That nickname properly depicted their color, yellow on the top half and white on the bottom. It was here that you would find my grandmother and grandfather (Madea and Bigdaddy), all seven of their children and a whole slew of their grandchildren. All of us, like many more of the poor black extended families, were right there together, packed in like sardines in a can. Some of us occupied the upstairs apartment and some occupied the downstairs apartment. This was a very beneficial set up on one hand in that it was easy for us to get to each other quickly when needed (especially when mama had to run upstairs to Madea to get away from daddy Paul when he started hitting on her). Also, if anybody in the family had a problem with somebody outside the family we could just go get the crew and the whole thing would get squashed, quickly. My family was always ready to fight. On the other hand, all of us being like sardines in that can gave way to some terrible family secrets. There was a demon that dwelt among us and he was able to hide under the lid of that 'sardine' can and transfer easily his influence from one of us to the next.

I was just about the youngest of the crew, an average 3-year-old that was full of life. I loved being outdoors and playing with all of my cousins most. Back then you know that children could roam free all day without too much worry about being taken. Nobody wanted us! I was a very open and carefree little girl. My cousin Metilda was about a year older than I was so she and I stuck together like best friends. Everyone else had a few years on us.

It wasn't an unusual thing for the adults in the family to leave all of the children alone at home together while they were off to work, maybe running errands on the weekends or simply out on the town for a night of fun. After all, there were definitely enough of us to keep each other. But that was the one benefit in my family, and in a lot of families across America, that proved to yield the bad results.

Now Ray Ray was the oldest cousin of us all and he was the one that I remember having the demon first. He was about ten years older than I was and I could tell that Metilda and I were his favorites to watch. Oftentimes right in the midst of one of our wild kid strides across the front yard, his tall, slim silhouette would appear at the screened door and he would call us both in. "Come here Marti and Metilda." He would always call only for us two. The others were left to continue to roam free and enjoy a full day of play without interruption. We reluctantly stopped our game of chase, not because we feared what was about to come, but just because we didn't want to stop playing. We were too young to fully comprehend what happened to us once we were on the other side of that door anyway. We obediently entered into the apartment and after he closed and locked the big wood door, were escorted into the bedroom. Being that we were just babies that couldn't stop nor understood what was going on, we were subjected to whatever he wanted to do to us, and he did just that; whatever he wanted to. Our childish minds were only

HOW IT ALL GOT STARTED

focused on getting back outside to play. He took turns with the both of us. With Metilda watching, he pulled my pants down to my ankles and had his way with me sexually. With my back to him, he pounded and pounded on me with his …you know…until he was ready to ask "the question". He would always ask me if I was ready for him to make something come out of him and onto me. I would hurry up and say yea because that meant that he was almost done with me and I could get back to playing. Then all of a sudden we both would become saturated with something 'wet'. That's all I knew that it was, wet. Metilda's turn would be next. Afterwards, he would make us take our usual naps together before we could return to play. Sometimes Metilda and I found ourselves rehearsing and replaying what he had just done to us on each other as we lay in bed together.

Ray Ray did this to us as often as our parents were away from home. So this was pretty much a continual thing. Our parents' worlds seemed to have been just too crowded with their own issues for them to notice that something was going on with us. Of course Ray Ray told us that it was our little secret and that we should tell no one, (shhh, don't tell nobody); and we didn't. It blows my mind when I think back about the times I use to complain to my mother about my private part hurting. Then after a trip to the doctor revealed the need for medication to be inserted inside me; no further discussion and no questions were asked. I've come to learn that for most families it's easier to ignore such issues and act as if nothing is going on, than to chance controversy and public humiliation for the family.

Imagine, if you will, yourself as a three-year old whose innocence is being stolen every opportunity by one whom should have been guarding it; by one with the same blood running through their veins as you. Now let's further complicate things by adding the stress of living in a small apartment filled with lots of violence. Some of you just might have to close your eyes and put forth great effort to picture all of this, but unfortunately too many of you know these experiences first hand. In conjunction with my experiences with Ray Ray, my mother, brother and I lived life everyday on pins and needles waiting for daddy Paul to fly off the handle again.

You see Paul was something like a gangster. He was a very loud, intimidating and violent man. He was big and muscular in stature, and could easily take down another above average man. His build, along with this aggressive personality led him to be named Douglas High School's star football player back in his school days. It was nothing to find rave reviews about him in the sports section of the newspaper, ranting about how great he was.

These very same qualities received a different connotation for him out in the streets however. Instead of ranting about how great he was it was said that he was a terrible, awful person. His ways earned him the nickname 'Killa' out in the streets and there was a whole lot of people afraid of him; out there, and at home. I was one of them! I guess a family could pride themselves on knowing that the man of their house could put an entire community in check, but we found out too that it's not necessarily good to have people walking around afraid of you. There was this one man that was so afraid of daddy that when Killa backed him in a corner just to talk, the man pulled out his pistol and shot him six times. He tried to make sure that Killa would die; but daddy was too mean for that. He kept right on living. When the doctors pulled all but one of those bullets out of him, he went right back to running the streets the very next day. They had to leave one bullet in him because of where it was; right in his buttocks. I think that God wanted him to always feel that pain in his ass to remind him of what a pain in everyone else's ass he had been.

Not only was daddy, himself, intimidating and scary, even his car was just as intimidating as he was. I swear that thing could move at speeds well over 100 mph and Killa drove at least that everywhere that we went. It was nothing for us to run into the back of the car in front of us as my brother Nathaniel and I sat nervously on the back seat. Back then there were no seat belt requirements so we just had to hold on for dear life the best that we could to whatever we could find to grab. The drivers of the two cars would get out to assess the damage. Daddy would say a few words and the other driver would fear the bass that he heard emanating from his voice and we would be off again at 100mph, no more questions asked. I use to be scared to ride the roller coasters at the old Liberty Land of Memphis, but the rides with daddy were much more scarier than the Zippin Pippin or any other roller coaster that I'd ever found myself on.

I could always tell when daddy was around the corner from the house in the evenings too. It seemed as if the sidewalks would begin to vibrate and I would get so nervous that my very soul began to tremble. Everything about this man made me nervous, but although I was afraid of him, I yet still thought of ways to try to keep him from coming home and beating on my mama. As soon as I saw him pull up and get out of his car I would run and jump up in his arms and just kiss all over his face to try to soothe his spirit. I tried to make him happy to keep him from jumping on mama since she couldn't seem to make him happy. I was willing to do whatever it took. Yes, whatever! My cousin was already teaching me things that seemed to make a man happy, and if that's what it took to calm my daddy, then I was willing to let him do it to me also. It turned out that daddy was a lot of things, but a pervert he was not. He had no interest in me and he simply peeled me off of him when he had had enough of my spit on his face and went found mama to, yes, pick a fight. There is a song that the Praise and Worship team at the Pursuit of God Transformation Center, sings that is so dear to me. It's entitled, "I Give Myself Away", (So You Can Use Me), by William McDowell. Every time I hear them sing that song my soul can't help but to break down and cry. I consider my state of mind back then, as merely a child, when I was willing to give myself to my earthly father sexually to use me to save my mother. I compare it to my state of mind today, willing to give myself to the heavenly father spiritually to use me to perhaps help save others who thought like me. What a transformed mind!

Sometimes, even mama would come outside when she heard daddy's old car pull up. Probably to determine what mood he was in and to beg him for the sake of her children not to come home clowning. Or maybe she just felt safer outside. It didn't matter to daddy

WHAT WAS MEANT FOR MY BAD...

though. He would fight inside or outside.

One day daddy made mama go inside one of the empty apartments since she had come outside. It would have been better for me if she had stayed inside and spared me the embarrassment of hearing the slaps against her face echoing through the apartment complex. I swear, I didn't know if my mother was going to walk out of there on her own or if I was going to have to go in there and get her myself. The spectators that had gathered definitely didn't want to get in Killa's business and help her. No one did as much as to even call the police on her behalf. I might have only been three years old, but I had readied my mind to go in there and bring my mama out. I just believed that I would have gotten enough strength somehow to get her out of there. Afterall, I was made strong.

I guess mama was strong too. She stayed with daddy and about a year or so later, they were having their third child. Bringing another baby in the house did not make things any better. As a matter of fact, things got so much worse that I very rarely slept at night. I now had another person that I had to look out for. I had to watch and listen for any signs of raised voices that might lead to a fight. I had to be ready to run in and try to save mama at a moment's notice. I stood posted at my bedroom's door at all times pacing back and forth. I recall one of the saddest things that I've ever had to listen to was the shrill screams of my mother as she was tortured by daddy Paul. With an unraveled clothes hanger dipped in the direct fire of a cigarette lighter daddy punished mama for not giving him "preferential sexual treatment" (if you know what I mean). I heard my mother insist she was not that kind of girl; but the heated metal that was pressed against her skin certainly was enough to turn her into that kind of girl. It was as if daddy was branding mama like a farmer would brand the cows on his farm.

As my older brother Nathaniel lay asleep in our bedroom (or pretended to be sleep), I stood by our bedroom door and listened. With tears rolling down my face, I begged God to help my mother. Now I had not yet had a live, personal experience with God. I had come to know of Him through the white people. The white people came on the 'joy bus' every week and picked up all us little black children in the hood and took us to their church. I don't know what church this was nor could I tell you the name of any of those people. I don't even remember their faces other than white. But as I prayed for mother, I didn't have time to wonder if this God that they were teaching me about was real. I just needed Him to be real right now and I needed Him to step in and do something. I loved my mother.

Afterwards, I became so protective of her that before she made it to one spot in the apartment, I was already there. If she started making her way to the kitchen, I was there too. Even when she went to the bathroom I tried to beat her there, but she would get there first and close the door on me. No matter though, I stood right outside that door like a little soldier in the army. I had appointed myself the lookout for Killa and I was determined not to let him get her. Mama knew that I was outside the door and in a very low and calm voice she would call, "Marti." When I answered timidly, "ma'am", she would scream, "get away from this door." She hated me following her around. It must have been heartbreaking to know that your baby girl's only concern in her young life was protecting you. I'm sure that she wanted me to focus on things that a child should have been focused on like playing with a doll or something. Or maybe she didn't hate me following her around after all, maybe she just hated me. I remember clearly the first time that I accepted that my mother did hate me. Mama sat on the couch to work on one of her number paintings (she loved to number paint), and I parked myself right under her armpit. I really needed to be close to her this particular day. I was feeling ill and needed that motherly attention. When she yelled at me for sitting next to her and made me move away, my mind flashed and took a mental picture of the hatred that I perceived that she had for me. The imprint of the hurt felt from being pushed away from her would remain on my brain forever. A feeling of rejection had just been deposited into my soul by the person that I had loved the most in the entire world. No matter though, I was a strong little girl.

◀ WHAT WAS MEANT FOR MY BAD...

I was taking blows like these in on a frequent basis and as if it all wasn't enough, life would pitch me yet another battle to deal with.

Mama eventually got a job working at the Market Basket over on Summer Avenue. You know that's like Easy-Way today. She decided to bring in a live in baby sitter to keep me during the day and to get Nathaniel off to school in the mornings. See, she had to be out of the house very early to catch her bus. Betty, who had no children of her own and in need of a place to stay, moved in. This set up was to be beneficial for us all.

Now let me remind you again that I was a very humble, timid, and nervous little girl at this point and wanted nothing more than to be loved by those who were supposed to love me. I minded everybody and gave no one a reason to hate me so far except for mama. But apparently Betty had a reason too. It was something in her that just flat out hated something in me. It seemed as though my very existence was reason enough for her to hate me, and she made me pay for existing every day. What she saw when she looked at me still remains a mystery to me until this day.

Betty was no small woman by any means. She was tall and very big boned and there was no escaping when she pounced on me trapping me in the headlock between her healthy thighs. She was like a lion on the hunt and I was her prey every time. She would beat me until her soul was satisfied or until she got tired, whichever came first. Her evil soul seemed to never get satisfied and her flesh did not tire easily. Too many days, I watched in despair as my mother went out the front door to work her job knowing that as soon as that door closed I was at the leisure of Betty.

At last, the physical signs of abuse began to show up. I began to have a nervous tremble about myself that I could not control. I started having problems with keeping my food down. Most times, after I'd finished eating, I would throw every bit of it right back up. No matter how hard I tried to control my nervous stomach and my tremble, I just couldn't. I knew that if I let my food come back up while Betty was there, a beating was the next thing to come. I soon learned to brace myself and prepare myself in my mind for her beatings. I told myself over and over again that I wouldn't let them hurt and I became immune to the physical pain, but there was no dodging the emotional torment. That, unfortunately, would stick with me for a life time. Sometimes, after breakfast, Betty would get me before she got Nathaniel off to school. He would have to witness the whole thing, but he was in no position to help me. He was just a child himself. We couldn't tell it because Betty told us not to or she would do something worse to us (Shhh, don't tell nobody). Anyway, I was already use to not telling. Ray Ray had taught me that.

Again I'll ask this rhetorical question, did I not display enough signs that something was wrong? Or did people just not care? Mama really should have known something wasn't right when one day she was cleaning and needed me to take my hair ribbons to my room and I refused. I just stood frozen in one spot shaking my head no to her. Stricken with fear, I couldn't talk to explain to her why. I just hoped that she would catch on. I had never been disobedient to her before, but I was just too afraid to go in that room this time. [I was like the little boy on the movie Ransom when he saw the man who had kidnapped him sitting in his own house. He was standing at his bedroom door stricken with fear as urine ran down his legs. His father immediately detected that something was wrong and took action to protect his son. But that was Hollywood. In real life in the hood, that little boy would have gotten a whipping for peeing on himself and embarrassing his daddy.] Betty was in my room listening to my mother as she told me to take the ribbons in there and shaking her balled fist at me daring me to come in. All while my mother was yet speaking. Mama threatened to whip me if I didn't go in. I, like mama had been when she got pregnant with me, was stuck between a rock and a hard place with no room to turn. I had a threatening person on each end and there I was in the midst. Mother didn't recognize that there was something wrong and it seems her only concern was exerting her parental power over me just for control.

Dealing with all of this as best as I could finally took a toll on me.

◀ WHAT WAS MEANT FOR MY BAD...

The stress of it all broke free and my nerves gave way to it. As I laid on my mother's couch in the living room, I began to have a nervous breakdown. My whole body trembled uncontrollably and I could not get it to stop. I can still hear the voice of my mother calling, "Marti, Marti", but I could not stop convulsing long enough to respond to her. I lay there and shook until I guess I drifted off to sleep.

To the doctors I went. EKG's and all kinds of other tests were run on me. I hated it when they left all of that glue in my hair because it hurt when mama combed it out. And I had a head full of hair to comb through too. They found that for some reason I had actual scar tissue left on a section of my brain. An injury had occurred some time ago and had already healed before anyone even knew it existed, (But God)! The doctors drew a picture for my mother to show her the location of the scars in case she had to tell another physician about them. They didn't know what exactly had triggered the convulsions nor what made me throw up all of the time so they referred to a mental therapist. It was referrals like these that led my own family to label me as crazy. You know when they put the index finger to the head and twirl it around. That was the stigma that became attached to me throughout my life. Even by the brother who had witnessed the terrible beatings that I suffered daily.

Somewhere along here Betty started working at a daycare center and had to take me with her. I wasn't actually enrolled at the center but they allowed Betty to bring me with her and they mixed me in with the other children anyway to allow her to work. During playtime some of the children were playing with the wooden blocks. You know the wood blocks with ABC on them. One of them threw a block and hit me in the head with it. When I threw it back and hit them, I was dragged off and put into a dark closet alone as punishment. Nothing of course happened to the other child. They must have thought that they were throwing me in their 'dungeon'. But actually it turned out that that was one of the best things that could have ever happened to me in my life. I was alone. I was secluded from everybody and for the first time I felt very safe. I had found sanctity in the closet. It was right there in that closet that I did have a live, personal encounter with God for the first time. You know that God that I didn't have time to wonder if He was real but just needed Him to do something earlier. Suddenly, I became aware that God was real and that I was not in the closet alone as I had supposed. There was something or someone in that closet with me. I could feel them. I couldn't see them and I couldn't touch them, but I felt them there. There was a presence that caused me to know peace in my mind. It made me want to sing and so I did. I lay on my back and looked towards the ceiling and imagined that I was in the sky with the stars. "Twinkle Twinkle Little Star" was the song that was in my heart. Now I know that that song is not a church song, but I will forever count it as my first praise and worship song unto the God that had made Himself real to me in that closet. In a situation where a child should have been trying frantically to get out of, God had filled me with a peace that made me wish I could stay there forever. The daycare workers thought that they were doing something bad but God made it a good thing unto me. Dottie Peoples said it best when she sang "the devil meant it for bad but I'm so glad God meant it for my good".

Now I don't want to lead you astray and I wish that I could tell you that I "lived happily ever after". That's fairy tale talk for me. No, my life did not instantly yield a miraculous turn of events. And I did not spend all of my days walking in Holiness and peace and harmony with God. In fact life would spew forth more battles between man and me and even spark a few spiritual fights between God and I before I would come to totally surrender to the Creator of all life.

-2-

The Transfer Of The Demon

MY BABYSITTING DAYS with Betty came to an end as I finally made it to the Kindergarten and joined my brother at Hollywood Elementary School. I can still remember walking to school with Nathaniel as he carried his big Bible every day. In my mind my brother was a preacher and I was proud of that. He wasn't going to have to use violence to put the neighborhood in check like daddy. He was going to use his Bible.

Ray Ray didn't keep me any more either. Nathaniel was big enough to watch me by himself now so mama left us at home alone when she had to be out of the house. We knew not to open the door for anybody and to put the television on the cartoons and sit there until she made it home, even if that took all day.

In school, I proved to be a very smart little girl excelling well above the other students at everything that the teacher taught. I was called on constantly in class to answer the most challenging questions that could be possibly posed by a kindergarten teacher, "What color is this crayon?" "C-A-T- spells what?" As smart as I was though, I had a hard time understanding why the next child couldn't even sing the alphabet song without messing it up. "What was wrong with these children?"

But I guess they asked the same question about me when my cup cake and chocolate milk came hurling out of my mouth everyday.

THE TRANSFER OF THE DEMON

"What is wrong with her", is what the puzzled looks on their faces said. You see, although I was now away from two major sources of affliction, the residue of abuse was still on me. The damage had been done and though my brain could hold it together academically it struggled trying to hold it together psychologically. Mama found herself coming to get me from school often because of that nervous stomach. They couldn't allow a vomiting child to remain at school and chance spreading a virus or something. Besides that, everything seemed to hurt me all the time now. My head hurt. My legs hurt. My eyes hurt. I even told mama one time that my blood hurt.

When mama had to come and get me early from school, she would sometimes take me to my aunt's house where my cousins would be home. They didn't have to go to school everyday. Their mother didn't always feel like getting up and getting them ready. Boy, they were lucky.

You do remember that I told you the demon that dwelt among us could easily transfer his influence from one of us to the next? Well that's exactly what happened when I was at their house. It was apparent that the devil was not through with me just yet. The bad spirit that Ray Ray had now somehow showed up in my cousin Ronnie, Metilda's very own brother. (And here I was thinking that Metilda and I were the only two that Ray Ray had gotten a hold to.)

Now Ronnie was only a few years older than I was so I actually hung out and played with him a lot more than the times that Ray Ray had kept me. As cousins and playmates, along with Metilda, we were around each other all of the time. There was no evidence that he would end up like Ray Ray until one day we played a game of mama and daddy. Now I know that everybody has played this game. But from what you can gather from this story line, you can just imagine what ended up happening in our game.

I didn't know what to say once Ronnie was on top of me. I just stared him in the face and waited for him to ask the question. You know the question that Ray Ray would ask me to let me know that he was almost done with me. Ronnie would always have his eyes closed

WHAT WAS MEANT FOR MY BAD...

and I figured that he kept them closed so that he wouldn't have to look at his little cousin and feel any guilt about what he was doing to her. What was he thinking as he used my body to satisfy his desires? Was he picturing my face or was he listening to the demonic voices in his head telling him that, "We are going to make her just like us one way or another?"

I wasn't sure either what I thought about Ronnie being on top of me but I do know that I felt different with him than I did with Ray Ray. I guess what made the difference was with Ray Ray, I had no true understanding as to what was going on. I didn't comprehend that I was being raped already of my innocence. Now that I was a little older, about six, I kind of knew about what Ronnie was doing and it was this knowledge (the knowledge of good and evil) that made me have some mixed-up and confused feelings.

At first, I enjoyed the physical touch of my cousin's hands on my body. That, of course, was the pleasure of the flesh. But after he was done I didn't feel so good. A feeling of embarrassment and shame had come over me as if the whole world had witnessed what we had done. I felt like that presence that had been in the closet with me at that daycare center showed up again and he was sort of fussing at me. And you should know by now that I didn't like to be fussed at. He caused me to think that I shouldn't let Ronnie do that to me. But I didn't know how to make him stop and I thought that it was just something that kin folks did with each other. I surely had learned not to tell (Shhh, don't tell nobody).

Anyway I made myself feel better by saying that everything that we had done was natural. All children played mama and daddy. I knew that because I had seen some of the other children in the apartments playing it too outside on a mattress. And everybody had sex. I knew that because we use to run around the apartments looking through the windows watching the grown ups do it. It seemed that there was nothing else for the down trodden people of the hood to do but have sex. I can imagine how a lot of the conversations must have gone, "Are you bored?" "Yes I'm bored" "Let's have sex!" "Are you hungry?" "Yes I'm hungry." "Let's have sex." Any reason was a good enough reason to have sex in the hood.

I sort of just "ignored" that chastisement by the presence from the closet about our little kid game of mama and daddy. But shortly after I ignored it, Ronnie started doing a new thing. He started… putting his tongue… between my legs and I knew for sure that that was grown up stuff. Ronnie had never done that to me before. I can't help but to wonder if I had found enough courage to make him stop in the beginning would I be testifying that my cousin was the first to perform oral sex on me. I thought my heart was going to pound right out of my chest. I wasn't sure though if it was from pleasure or from fear. It made me think about that night when daddy had tortured mama because she wouldn't do this to him and here I was having it freely done to me by my own cousin. I could understand clearly the power that daddy must have imagined himself having over mama because I myself had walked into an unsolicited power that caused my cousin to bow unto me.

-3-

The Move From The Hood

WELL, MADEA EVENTUALLY got her a house and got up out of the 'hood' (thank God). She moved, along with all of my aunts, onto Barbara Drive off of Jackson Avenue. As for my mother, she decided to hang around in the Yellow and Whites hoping that things would get better between she and Killa. Things never did and when she got tired of him hitting on her we eventually joined the rest of the family too.

The new house was a two family dwelling with about five families living in it, Madea and all of her girls and all of their children. I didn't care that we all were living in this one house together again. I was just glad that we had left Killa, Betty and my cousin Ray Ray behind. Come to find out, after we left, it was said that Betty was seen walking up and down the streets pushing a stroller with a doll in it like it was a real baby. God had taken her mind like the demon in her thought he was going to take mine (or maybe her mind was already gone before she even moved in with us). Ray Ray was my uncle's boy and he didn't make the move with us either. He did make a move to the big house though for doing the bad things that he did out in the streets. Maybe, just maybe things would get better for me and I would have a chance of living a normal and healthy child's life now.

With twenty of us in the house, and with only four bedrooms, we had to sleep three or four to a bed. Metilda and I usually slept in the bed with my Aunt Gertrude.

THE MOVE FROM THE HOOD

Although my new home life was no longer filled with violence and I no longer had to stand my post listening for the threat of a fight all night, sleeplessness was still in control. While we had left behind some of the enemy's star players on his team, there was one who packed up and transferred himself right to Barbara Drive with us. My tormentor! I was now terrified to fall asleep at night because the first night that I did the tormentor put the tip of his finger under my nose and caused my breath to cease. Let me explain. I just stopped breathing at night. Imagine that! During the middle of the night I would loose my breath and wake up gasping for air. It was as though someone was actually ciphering the very breath from my nostrils. I can still remember clearly as if it was last night, mama, grandma, and auntie rushing me into the bathroom and beating me in my back trying to make me breathe. As hard as I tried to take in the slightest of air, I just couldn't. Night after night this happened. Each time I felt that it would be my last time. I thought that I was going to collapse and die right there in the bathroom on the floor with my folks standing over me. I'd always visualized my cousins running in looking in my stiff face with my eyes wide open, (you see I don't like to close my eyes), and then one of them suddenly shouting out "Dam, Marti dead!" My cousins would say little curse words like that from time to time when something exciting happened. But Marti wasn't dead. God didn't see fit to let me die on that bathroom floor. And after Madea called on the name of her Lord, air began to flow into my body again.

Well, I lived. And I lived long enough to meet myself a new friend from my new neighborhood. I started spending a lot of my time playing with my new best friend Tina. Her family lived on Barbara Drive also. There was something different about Tina just like there was something different about me. We seemed to have both been 'black sheep'. She didn't have a lot of friends and wasn't a very pretty girl at all just like I wasn't. [The children at school had made sure to let me know how ugly I was. They teased me everyday saying that my lips looked like they had been hanging on a rusty nail and was swollen with infection. They *were* huge though in comparison to my child sized head and face.] Any way, Tina wore a teeny weenie afro, had dark blotchy skin and was kind of fat. But I guess that I liked her because she was of the rejected sorts like me. I liked my new friend. A lot! My like actually turned into an attraction and I found myself wanting to do the same things to her that Ronnie and Ray Ray had done to me. And I did. Tina and I became like girlfriends. I don't mean two little girls that were friends. I mean literal girlfriends. I had my first girlfriend at the age of eight. (Naw, Metilda couldn't have been my first girlfriend because she was my cousin.) Whenever Tina and I found ourselves alone in a room, whether at her house or mine, we "made love" to each other. This is when I first realized that I was truly going to be gay. Now I hear a lot of people say that they were born gay but this is what makes me beg to differ. I believe that, as in my case, after they were born, a homosexual seed of some sort was planted in their life, and that seed was allowed to germinate and grow. Ray Ray had used Metilda to plant the seed within me. Think back to when she and I rehearsed what he had done to us on each other. We were practicing homosexuality at three and four years old. There was no one available to kill that spirit and so it took root inside of us. Right now today there are men and women planting homosexual seeds by molesting little boys, telling them that they are sissies, and by raping little girls causing them to hate men and pushing them towards the security of another female. Some of these little boys or girls may have been so young that they can't recall the moment of deception so they believe that they were born that way.

Anyway, I still had my cousin Ronnie in the picture also, so I guess that actually made me bisexual. No, confused is an even better word. I would battle for many years with whether I wanted to be straight or gay; whether I *was* straight or gay, or bi.

Ronnie's mother eventually moved out of Madea's big house. She moved out and took her four children (Raymond, my Ronnie, my Metilda and Albert) back off of Springdale Street onto Piedmont. Even though we didn't live everyday together anymore, I still had them whenever mama would let me spend the night with them; when I

THE MOVE FROM THE HOOD

begged her hard enough. You know how you use to beg and plead with your mama to let you spend the night at your cousin's on the weekends, and I was begging extra hard because I knew that I had something to look forward to. (Was I a bad girl?)

When bedtime came over on Piedmont, I could hardly fall asleep, being filled with anticipation. I would lie on my pallet that I had made for myself on the floor, pretend to be sleep and wait for Ronnie to climb on top of me. And sure enough, like clock work, he did. My emotions shot all over the place. I would guess that I was like a drug addict, loving and enjoying the pleasure of the high but barely tolerable of the crash that followed. My flesh was definitely warring against my spirit and I wasn't sure at all which of them I wanted to win. To be truthful, I think that I started to become pro flesh. Confusion continued to increase within me and before I knew it I was crying myself to sleep regretting that I had let him do it to me. Surprisingly though, by the time the next weekend came I was begging mama to let me spend the night again. I didn't even care that once he got off of me, that he went and climbed on top of his own sister. Metilda and I was in this thing together. The enemy of my mind had me on his hook and he could reel me in whenever he wanted to. Anyway, that would all take place on the week-ends and only when mother allowed me to stay.

During the course of the week I had the neighborhood crew to play with. We ripped and ran until the evening was to come to an end. And it was at the ending of the evening when I would realize that my mama wasn't home. Because I loved my mother, I worried all of the time when she wasn't there. It didn't matter to me that she didn't like me very much. If she hadn't made it in by a certain time, my nervous condition would kick back up again. That little army soldier mentality that I had developed earlier on crept back up as the tormentor of my mind yielded forth mental images of my mother lying bloody on the side of the road. I remember trying to send my spirit to where I thought she was, pick her up off that street and bring her home. I never could make it to her though.

My Aunt Gertrude and Aunt Freda could always tell when I was worrying because I would begin to pace back and forth. From the dining room to the living room, peeking out of the windows like that old nosy next door neighbor that watched everything. My aunts always tried to console me by reassuring me that my mother would be walking through the door at any moment.

I could always tell how late she was running by the color of the sky. If the sun had started to leave the sky but there was a little purple like tint outside (sunset), then she had a couple of more minutes to make it in. I would pray for her as I paced through the house. But once that sky got black and she wasn't there, I would run and hide in the closet and begin to beg God to, "please send my mama home safely."

By this time it would be dinner time and my Aunt Gertrude would have my plate fixed along with the other children. While they were eating their pinto beans and cornbread, however, I would be in the closet. Someone would ask, "Where's Marti?" my aunt would say, "In the closet. You know she's not going to eat until Annette gets here." It was only when I heard my mother's voice that I came out with a tear stained face happy that she was home. Then and only then would I eat my cold supper. Of course I was sitting at the table by myself by now. All the other children had long finished their meals and were probably getting ready for the bed. But I was happy.

God always answered my prayers concerning the safety of my mother and I was thankful to have my knowledge about who He was expanded even after we left the Yellow and Whites. We started going to church with Grandma Alice, Paul's mother. She would pick us up every Sunday and take us to Summerfield Missionary Baptist Church, on Boxwood and Chelsea where Reverend W. W. Mitchell was the Pastor. One day as I listened to Reverend Mitchell preach I began to tell God how much I loved Him and that I wanted to live my life for Him forever. I remember sitting on that wooden pew in church vowing to myself that I would always love God no matter what happened to me. The thought came to my mind that, "Even if a lawnmower's blade shot off and put my eye out I would still live for God. I would just walk around and preach with a black patch on my eye." (Lord I hope that I wasn't prophesying). I just found a great pull on me to do God's work. When Reverend Mitchell opened the doors of the church, I felt something tug at me. It kept tugging at me until it pulled me right up in front of the congregation. As everyone looked on, I publicly believed in my heart, confessed with my mouth, repented of my sins, and asked to be baptized. You know those are the steps you take in the Baptist church to get saved. I surprised even myself by going up there considering how timid and shy I was. I was so shy that I could never even say my Easter speeches on Easter Sundays. Every time It was my turn to say my speech, when I got up there, the words just wouldn't come out. Mama had to come get me down year after year. But I knew this feeling. I *was* this feeling. The words that Pastor Mitchell spoke out of his mouth came to life within me. "In the beginning was the Word, and the Word was with God, and the Word was God...And the word was made flesh, and dwelt among me" (St. John 1:1, 14). It was the Word that was calling me to the front and I had to respond to it.

I was eight years old when I got baptized and I was for real about serving God. I was so for real that all of the other children in the house stopped playing with me. If, while they were reading adult books filled with bad words, I came into the room they would hurry up and close the book. "Don't let Marti see", someone would shout. "oohhwee, yall in here looking up bad words", I shouted. Everything that they did wrong, I was right there to tell them that God didn't like it. But I was still ignorant to the fact that He didn't like what I was doing either and what I was letting other people do to me. But I had already had that seed planted in me and as I would discover, it would not easily be uprooted. For one thing, there were just not enough good, responsible adults back then who taught about sexual immoralities. There seemed to have been only child molesters who said "shhh, don't tell nobody" or parents and grandparents who didn't discuss sex at all and said "shhh, don't talk about that.". But one day, God let Reverend Mitchell do it. He actually talked about sex. In church! And he was talking to me! (and probably some others too.) I'll never forget his words. He said, "You got eight year olds running around here knowing more about sex than I do, masturbating and everything". "How did he know that?", I wondered. Well, God is the one who actually knew that and He used the preacher to send me the message. It was important that I knew right then that I was on a destructive path. "How shall they hear without a preacher?" (Romans 10:14).

So now at this point, not only was my family subjected to hear about God from me, but even when I played with the other children in the neighborhood, they had to hear about Him too. They would pick games to play like hide & go seek, not it or tag. When it was my turn to choose, I chose church. It was about five or six of us that hung in a group and I would form them into a little choir. I of course would be the choir director. I taught them the childhood favorite of mine, "I love to praise Him". I would have my friends rocking on the front porch and because I did, I felt that God was very pleased with me. By the time I made it to the fifth grade, the school children were calling me 'that sanctified girl'. I didn't talk much at school so how all those children picked up sanctification in my soul, I don't know. Would you believe too that by now my mother had started dressing me like a little girl and all I wore was dresses. So that added to their belief that I was really sanctified. My school teacher took it upon herself to modify my name to Mardyam Andrea to make it more feminine. She changed it on all my paperwork at school and that's been my name ever since. There was not one question raised about the new 'misspelling' of my name, not even by my own mother. God had allowed the name modification for me and that was final.

-4-

Another Bad Home

TIME PASSED ON and mama of course started to date again. She brought a couple of her new boyfriends home to meet the family and I guess that these guys were all right and all, but no serious relationship ever developed with them. Until one day she brought Frederick home. He was extremely nice and seemed to be very peaceful the same way that I imagine Samuel must have been towards her at first. But what I really liked most was that not only did he come to visit mama when he stopped by, but he also included us. He would take us riding in that long white Lincoln Continental with that CB antenna on the back. I remember having fun imitating him as he talked on that thing, "Breaker breaker good buddy. That's a big ten four", whatever all of that meant. He drove the speed limit so we didn't have to worry about running in the back of somebody during our course of travel like we had with Paul.

We would often go to Dairy Queen for ice cream cones at night and sit out under the umbrellas on the store's patio. Sometimes we even stopped at Tops Bar-B-Que for a burger. Those were the best cheeseburgers around during the time. They were huge too, but that was back then. Things were looking up for us now and I was happy for my mama. Frederick had exactly what mama needed, love and affection, and mama had exactly what Frederick wanted.

I had heard mama say that it was time for us to move out on our own again. We all were getting bigger and older and madea's house was growing too small for all of the different personalities that were evolving. Besides that, I'm sure that she was eager to have a place where she and Frederick could spend more time together, understandably. I was all right with that. Like I said, things were going real good and I really liked Frederick.

One day while I was out playing (probably preaching to somebody), I saw a duplex house for rent on the next street over from where we lived. I was so excited that I ran home as fast as I could and told mama to come look at it to see if she liked it and if we could get it. This would be our chance to live as our own little family again. She came and checked it out and she was quite impressed by what I had done. she really did like the duplex. Boy, I think that was like the high light of my life. I had done something that actually made mama very happy.

Shortly afterwards we found ourselves moving in on Biggs Street. Since it was only one street over from where we were moving from, we would still be by our family.

After we moved in and got settled, it wasn't long before Frederick was staying with us. At first it was just a casual overnight stay with him gone before we woke up (supposedly). They must have forgotten that I was the General on watch in the household. I knew what time he came and what time he left.

Frederick seemed to have thought a lot of me. He thought that I was very special and he wanted to be close to me. Mother probably told him how sickly I had been in the past and he probably just wanted to help me get better. Likewise, I thought of him as a very gentle person that would be good to have around for all of our sakes. Everybody could be at ease. No more loud raised voices. No more fear dominating the environment.

Frederick did spend a lot of time playing with me. I figured that since I was the only girl that he didn't want me to feel left out when he and the boys did things together. His favorite thing to do seemed to be to tickle and wrestle with me. He would tickle me under my neck as he flipped me on the floor, and I must admit, it was great taking in all of that fatherly love and attention. There were no threats of beatings ever.

He tickled me on my chest. He tickled me under my arms. He tickled me… hum. Now that could have been questionable. He tickled me some more. Then one day there was an accident. His hand accidentally slipped between my legs. "Sure, it was just a slip of his hand", I made myself think. This man was crazy about my mother and me and there's no way possible that this was about to play out like the thought that flashed in my head. But I guess that since the questionable tickle was not checked when it first happened, that gave way for all the other tickles to sure enough became tickles with malicious intent. Frederick had soon figured out that I had been trained not to tell and so his tickles eventually turned into gentle messages on my chest and between my legs. I absolutely abhorred the French kisses that were soon added. The saga of my life's journey began to pick up momentum again. The demon had transferred again and just was determined to not leave me alone. I determined in my heart that I would not destroy my mother's joy by telling her that something as crazy as this was happening to me. I decided that I would just take it for the sake of my mother. After all, God had made me strong.

Mother and Frederick were eventually married and she had not one clue about the monster that she vowed that we would spend the rest of our lives with. Remember that I told you earlier that my mother had something that Frederick wanted? Well he had worked his way in until he had complete access to it. Wedlock had definitely given him total access to and parental control over me, day and night.

Frederick started telling me how much he thought about me. He wrote letters expressing how he wanted to be closer to me than he already was. I couldn't phantom how much more closer a father could have gotten to his daughter. I thought that we were too close already.

Mama even granted him the privilege of tucking his new baby girl into bed at night as she busied herself in their bedroom, probably preparing her own self for the return of her lover. He usually was the last

WHAT WAS MEANT FOR MY BAD...

one I saw before crying myself to sleep, again, after he'd fondled me for quite some time. My 'goodnights' were usually filled with extended tongue kisses that I dreaded and sly touches on my breasts that left me with a sick empty feeling of death. I was only about nine years old and couldn't imagine why my underdeveloped breasts would excite a grown man to such a degree. Naturally, I no longer liked him and his presence only added to my emotional distress. But again I played big girl and took whatever he dished out. I was not going to mess this up for my mama. Being a big girl did come with a price you know. I suffered everyday. The flow of my tears seemed unstoppable. I never closed my eyes for watching for his shadow to approach my bedroom door. Then when my eyes were tired of being open and they shut on their own, my body began to convulse causing them to fly open again. So I lay in my bed with my eyes wide open until I drifted into unconsciousness as I exclaimed scriptures from the Bible, " The Lord is my shepheard; I shall not want... Yea, though I walk through the valley of the shadow of death, I will fear no evil: for thou art with me..." (Psalm 23). I got up the next morning only to repeat the same cycle of events from the previous day.

I was attending Berclair Elementary School and was in the fifth grade now. God had given me great intellectual abilities and I made nothing but A's. Every six weeks when the principal's list came out, there my name was at the top of it. By the time I made it to the sixth grade, the whole school had come to expect greatness from me. It was nothing for me to walk past even the bus drivers as they lined the street waiting for their bus riders to fill the buses and hear a conversation about me. "There goes the smartest kid in the school", they would say. And then my bus driver would say, "Yes, and she rides my bus." They were all so proud of me and not one of them had the slightest hint that I was suffering in my home everyday.

Time passed on and on my 11th birthday, my mother sent Frederick and I to the store to get me some stockings to wear to church. Imagine my shock when we pulled up to a hotel. "What is this all about?", I asked myself. I had no clue what was going on but

I felt very uncomfortable. Maybe we were going to stop by to visit some of his friends who were hanging out at the hotel. Maybe there was a surprise party planned for me and when we go in, everyone will jump out and yell, 'surprise'. "Lord please let that be the reason we're here". I had no time to prepare for a party though. I had big rollers in my hair and I was chewing and popping a piece of bubble gum like a big kid. "Stop popping that gum like that before the man at the desk think that you're a baby", he told me. It was all right with me if he did notice that I *was* just a baby. Maybe his heart would be filled with compassion enough to rescue me.

He bought and paid for the room and we went in. If I didn't know any better, I would think that I had been set up by my own mother. How could she not know what this person was capable of? Where does the comfort to take a child, your own step-child, to a hotel room to have sex come from? Did it ever run across his mind that I just might tell my mother, and if it did was there not enough fear of what she would do to keep him from this? Evidently not!

There was absolutely no one in the room except he and I and absolutely no good explanation as to why we were there. There we were, just the two of us. Frederick and I. What could possibly be going on here? He cut the television on and when he did all I saw were women kissing and getting it on with each other. More homosexual seeds being planted in my mind. There were about three of them in the group, all of them doing what they wanted to do to the other one. Frederick stretched himself across the bed and motioned for me to lie on the bed beside him. Then it dawned on me. He had previously told me that whenever I thought I was ready to have sex to let him know. He said that he wanted to be the first to show me what it was like, the same as he had did for Ebony, his first stepdaughter from a previous marriage. I don't remember telling him that I was ready to have sex, but I guess he was ready for me to be ready.

I didn't know how he was planning for us to get started. Was he just going to jump on top of me like Ronnie or did he expect for me to pull my own clothes down like with RayRay. I was still barely an eleven-year-old girl that day but I began to act and cry like a baby. I do mean loud with big crocodile tears rolling down my face. This just could not happen. "God please don't let me be taken by this grown man", I prayed. I didn't want this to happen. I cried so loudly that it must have scared him. He had a change of heart and hurriedly got me out of there. I guess he thought that someone was going to hear me and come to see about me. Yeah right! Unfortunately, one thing that I have learned in this life is that people don't come to see about you. They read about you in the news when it's too late and say, "umhum, I knew something was going on over there all the time. Po child!". They talk about you when they see you walking the streets selling your body saying, "that's a crying shame", after it was them that didn't come to see about you while your father was touching your private parts when you were a kid. They shake their heads at you when you get trapped in an abusive relationship that could claim your life at any time. The old folks use to say that it takes a village to raise a child. Villages now-a-days have diminished so that children are basically raising themselves the best that they know how.

Well after being gone for several hours, we finally made it back home. I don't know if we had the stockings or not. I really don't remember buying any and I think we told mama that the store had closed. I was cool as a cucumber going into the house and said not a mumbling word about where we had been. I acted like nothing had happened. Hell, I was use to this. Mother did surprisingly wonder what had taken us so long, but whatever lie Frederick told her gave her contentment.

I started to wonder if something similar to what he was doing to me had happened to him when he was child. After a peculiar incident at his parents' house, this suspicion was increased. His parents were elderly and his father was actually on his deathbed at this time. Often times they would take us with them when they went to check on his parents. They were a very quiet couple but I could tell that his mother didn't think very much of us. She thought that we were from the slums and that my mother wasn't good enough for her son. I can't understand how someone living on Shasta Street in the Hollywood area where the alcoholics, drug dealers and prostitutes maintained the corners, could think that they were better than the next person. Frederick's father was much more down to earth and accepted us better than his mother.

One day the father called me into his room. He was in a hospital bed and had oxygen tubes running into his nose. They had literally sent him home to die. His father motioned for me to come into his bedroom and out of the respect that I had for him, I did. He handed me a little AM/FM radio. It was nice and I really appreciated it because I really didn't have much. He motioned for me to bend down and give him a hug and when I did he fondled my breast and actually commented, "just feeling the tits." Why should I have expected anything differently? Shock and disbelief consumed me. I allowed numbness to take over me right then. I didn't want to feel anything any more and I didn't want to consider what had just happened to me. This was just all too much for me to try to rationalize. Why was my God, the God that I vowed to love and do His work, letting this happen to me and how much did He think that I could take? For goodness sakes I was only eleven years old.

I certainly didn't think that I could take any more and decided that I would just end this life here on earth. When I made it home, I went to the bathroom and started cutting on my wrist and fingers with a razor blade. I begged and pleaded with God to let me come and live with Him. I was really kind of hoping that He would intervene and just stop the beat of my heart naturally so that I wouldn't feel the pain of the cuts being made on my wrists. He intervened all right. He sent my mother right on in the bathroom and she caught me cutting myself. More indications to them that I was crazy. She chastised me of course, but it still wasn't enough for her to get the picture that something was going on.

Our lives went on as it had been and when I turned fourteen, I was presented with a brown paper bag. It had a gift inside for me from Frederick. I was a little leery about getting gifts from him. Usually

WHAT WAS MEANT FOR MY BAD...

when I got gifts from him, it cost me something. He bought me a Rubik's cube when they first came out. After I let him touch all over my body and grind himself against me for it, he replied, "Is that all that you're gonna give me?" He actually wanted me to have sex with him for a Rubik's cube. If I was going to become a whore, he wasn't going to be able to get me for a dam Rubik's cube. So, already nervous and suspicious about his gifts and his expected payments, I peeked inside the bag. I had no idea what the oblong shaped object was. "What's this," I asked him. "It's something to keep the bumps on your face cleared up", he responded. It was a vibrator. "It's a what?" "A vibrator", he said. Of course I still had no idea what it was nor what to do with it. He demonstrated how to turn it on and he let me feel the vibration on my fingers and even though I didn't want him to use it on me, I think I was a little curious about it and was willing to try it myself. We decided to just leave it in the bathroom's closet hidden behind the sheets way in the back for me to use at my discretion. This all would be just between he and I (Shhh, don't tell nobody).

My curiosity was raised and not only did I play around with that vibrator, but I started experimenting with other things also. Demonic seeds were being dropped all throughout my spirit and they would take root and grow, manifesting themselves through one form of perversion or another.

Little did we both know that I would inadvertently share this secret with somebody that I would meet at school and everything would be exposed. I spent my 9th grade year at Cypress Jr. High School. The school board had rezoned the school's districts and moved us from Snowden Elementary where I went for my 7th and 8th grade school years to Cypress. I started to come out some this particular school year. I wasn't as shy as I previously had been. I actually think that I was becoming numb to life. I tried out for the majorette team at the school and of course made it. I started using my middle name and became known as Andrea instead of Mardyam. I even got my first real boyfriend. You know the ones that mama allow to come over only when she's home. His name was Rowland. He was a drummer for the majorette squad and I tell you he and all those young black boys surely knew how to make those drums talk, especially to me. I mean they were filled with rhythm that seemed to have come straight from the mother land; Africa.

Performing on the majorette team was as natural to me as breathing during the day, not at night. You see I was born a dancer and I loved music. It was imbedded in my bones. Just like how some people feel that they were born gay, well I was born with the gift of dance in me. One day we had a school jamboree and the majorettes had to perform. We did our thing on stage, and we did it quite well. We had a really good majorette team. After we were done and were marching out of the auditorium that gift that I was born with manifested itself. I turned around, marched back down that aisle by myself and turned the school out. My dancing style was very seductive. (I think that it had always been that way.) I danced my way around the auditorium and right up to the principal. I left him in awe when I had finished rolling, dropping and shaking all up on him. I broke him down in front of the entire school. It was all student-principal friendly though. All of the students loved it and were chanting my name, "An-dre-a, An-dre-a" with their hands thrown in the air, waving them from side to side. I became 'their' majorette. But I couldn't understand why when I made it back to my health class my teacher was flabbergasted and appalled. She said that she was shocked at my sluttish behavior and display of filth. She consulted with a couple of other teachers to try to have me expelled. What was her problem? I really didn't know what I had done wrong. Mama said that I had been dancing like that since before I could walk, and friends and family always asked me to dance for them. Besides that, our majorette instructor was Peaches, and everybody know that he-she didn't expect anything less than the best and I was able to give it to him-her, whatever Peaches was. (See Peaches had some of those seeds planted in him that were allowed to germinate and grow. I don't know what to call him-her.) Every majorette team has a peaches though.

Now that I think back, I remember that my dancing even made

daddy Paul happy back in the day. He would make me dance for him when he was in a good mood. He would play that theme song to S.W.A.T. (from the 70's or maybe before) and I would just run from room to room in that apartment back in the Yellow and Whites dancing. I couldn't have been any more than about 2 years old, but I brought enjoyment to everybody when I danced (except for my health teacher apparently).

Well, I wasn't expelled from school and neither was I kicked off the squad. I was a bad (in a good way) girl. The majorette practices in the evenings gave me a way of escape from home for a little while and I especially enjoyed walking home with Rowland after the practices. Our walks home were usually uneventful and we just talked about what 9th graders talked about. Largely, I used this time I shared with him as my calm before the storm because I knew that once I made it home my peace would be gone.

One particular day, my calm was prematurely interrupted. As we walked the corner of Biggs (the street that my house was on) and Vollentine, a gang of boys pulled up beside us in a car. One jumped out and pointed a gun at my head. "Lord have mercy", I thought. "What is this?" The dude asked Rowland, "man this yo woman?" Rowland said "yeah". "Man she was with me last night, with my partner over there the night before and my other partner before that. I'm gonna kill this bitch right here", he shouted. I fell to the ground with my hands clasped around my head and waited for the bullet to pierce through. I finally broke my silence with "God please" and instantly the guy that was driving the car peeled off down the street. The boy with the gun then took his focus off of me and chased behind them in the car ordering them to stop and threatening to shoot the back windows out. They stopped to let him in and they all drove away. I had never seen these guys before in my life. They could have easily killed me right then, but God! I just got up and walked home like nothing happened. Didn't tell mama, didn't call the police. I had it figured by now that this was the kind of treatment that my life warranted. I guess I should have been happy that God didn't let him shoot me. And I was. The last thing I would have wanted was to have my neighbors bent over looking down at me and then have one shout out, "Damn, she dead" as they shake their head and walk away.

After that incident Rowland walked me all the way home and would stay in my house until it was close to the time for my mother to get home. Just like for us all when we were growing up, I wasn't supposed to have company in the house when no one was there. One time Rowland stayed in the house too long and we got caught. He was sitting in the swivel chair which sat right by the door and I was sitting on the floor in front of the chair, at his feet. We honestly had not done any mischief but never-the-less he wasn't supposed to have been in there. Frederick came home early and there we were. I think that's the first time that I ever heard him fuss and get angry. He didn't even fuss when he caught my brother in the actual act with his girlfriend. And here I was just sitting on the floor doing nothing. After he fussed at me, rebellion rose on the inside and I told Rowland that he was just jealous seeing us together. Rowland wondered why a father would be jealous over his daughter's boyfriend. I then told him what had been going on at home. I even let him read one of the letters that Frederick had given me. He of course tried to get me to tell it then. "What, are you crazy? I'm not going to take my mother's happiness away", I said. We bickered back and forth about it as I tried to convince him not to say anything.

As time passed on I must admit that bitterness started to settle within me. This situation had caused Rowland and I to fight and I was starting to just get sick and tired of the whole thing.

One day, I took the letter that Frederick had written to school with me. I guess I was trying to decide if I was going to tell it or not. Rowland was still pushing me to tell. He had said that if I didn't tell it, he was going to. The pressure from it all had built up so much that during lunch I just hit the floor. I passed out. When they got me up and to the office I just handed the school authorities the letter. I didn't have to say a word. That was it. Everything was exposed and out of my hands. Immediately and without me knowing, the school contacted

◄ WHAT WAS MEANT FOR MY BAD...

the Department of Children Services (DCS). They had also contacted my aunt Gertrude and told her what was going on. I was shocked when she walked through that office door. Everything was moving so fast and I couldn't control nor stop it. My aunt took me home with her because I could not return to my house. I couldn't go to my house as long as Frederick was there while the investigation was going on. By the time we did get home, DCS had already been by my house and stuck an investigation letter in the mailbox. They were ready to take action and all hell was about to break loose! I felt like a war was raging and I didn't know who was friend or foe. Can you guess where I was when the darts started flying later on that evening? You are right, in the closet. I was somehow looking for that peace that I had found in my first closet experience but I couldn't find it. Everything was chaotic in my head. My heart pounded extremely hard and fast. My thoughts couldn't form. All of a sudden my tongue was real cold like life was leaving me. I really wished that I would just die and I did again beg God to take me away from it all. Let me die right there in that closet. I didn't need anybody hovering over me saying, "Damn, she dead." I would not have cared if they never figured out that I was dead. I could have been like Enoch in the Bible that God just took. Sadly, all I could think about was how I must have hurt my mother. How could I be so low down and take all of this away from her.

Well, I didn't die and I had to eventually come out of the closet and face mama to explain everything that had happened. My Aunt took me home while Frederick wasn't there and I had to talk to mama. She cried and I cried. The more she cried, the more I cried. Nathaniel had left home by now and joined the Army. He had just so happen to call home. He heard us crying and couldn't help but to cry himself. I think he was more angry about it all than mother. I had devastated my mother and I hated myself for it. But at least now it was all out and she could wrap her loving arms around me and finally make me safe. Mother wasn't capable of that though. Just when I was expecting her to say that everything would be all right now, she assured me of just the opposite. She looked me dead in my eyes, pointed her finger and exclaimed "you are a liar and when I find out for sure that you're lying on him you've got to get up out of here." Whoa! What the hell. I *was* in hell. Where was I going to go? I was only fourteen. I went on to tell her about the vibrator that he had bought me. She argued her point that he had bought that vibrator for her. She knew that it was in the closet the whole time. "Then how on earth was it, mother that I knew about it too?" Either way, what kind of conversation was this for a mother to be discussing with her fourteen- year old daughter. Arguing over a vibrator that a low down man had brought in the house. I'm sorry. For the sake of the purpose of this book, let me rephrase that sentence. Arguing over a vibrator that a demon possessed individual had brought in the house. I even told her about the hotel. By then I think that she had stopped listening to me though. Frederick was right. There was no reason for him to fear the possibility of me telling my mother the things that he had done and he knew it.

DCS finally said that one of us had to leave the home. Clearly mother didn't want Frederick to leave and I didn't want to live with anyone else. I was much too timid to live with someone else. I probably would have spent the rest of my life in closets for sure. To hold everything together and to make it all stop, I became that liar that my mother said I was and said that Frederick hadn't done anything wrong. Mother was much happier having to drag me to St. Peter's Home for Girls for counseling every week-end than having to let Fred go. You see, now I had a bad reputation as a trouble maker with issues and was ordered to counseling sessions at St. Peter's Village. But the truth was that I had been a victim of rape, molestation and abuse and just wanted somebody to make it all stop.

While I didn't lock myself in my actual closet at home, I did lock myself in my room. I became extremely withdrawn from every body in the house including my little brother. I barely came out to eat and the times that I did were the times that mama made me.

I did eventually muster up enough rebellion to ask mother if I could go and live with my daddy though. Periodically when I would have my angry spells I would throw this question at her. I guess that I

◂ WHAT WAS MEANT FOR MY BAD...

must have asked mama one too many times about living with daddy 'cause the next thing that I knew her fist was pounding me upside my head. Boy, why was she so angry about such a reasonable request? I would find out some years later that my "daddy" request wasn't quite so reasonable after all.

-5-

Mo Money (Mo Problems)

WE MOVED THAT summer to Frayser. Things slacked up with Frederick because DCS was on the case and instructed him not to discuss anything sexual with me any more. They told him to leave the talks about the birds and the bees up to my mother. They may as well have told him to let me learn about it on my own. The only thing that I didn't like at home at this point was seeing Frederick walk around the house in his underwear. I hated being subjected to his bulging private business in his drawers. But it didn't seem to bother Mama that he walked around this way.

Well, I considered Frayser an upgrade from the neighborhood we had moved from. We had bought our own house and like the Jeffersons, we were "moving on up."

I started my tenth grade year at Frayser High School. Of course I met a whole new group of people and friends. The school wasn't far from the house so I walked there and back. One day, while walking home, I had an intriguing conversation with one of the school's finest and sexiest students that existed. You see it had rained, and there were lots of worms that had washed up on the sidewalks. I didn't want to step on them and feel them squash under my feet, so I was tiptoeing and jumping over them as I walked down the street; minding my own business. "If you're scared of those little worms, I know you're scared of the big worms too." (Now where was that little still voice that was supposed to have spoken into my spirit and told me to run? Just know that anybody that starts a conversation like that can't mean anybody else any good. So ladies, I will be your small still voice and tell you to RUN!) Umm... But he looked too good to run away from though. And boy was he smelling good too. The best dressed 10th grader in the school was actually talking to me. He was wearing a white cashmere coat; in the rain. His jerry curl was always fresh and his gold tooth sparkled every time he smiled. "You talking to me", I asked. "I don't see nobody else out here jumping over worms". Well all it took was a little more conversation and needless to say, before you knew it he had me on his hook. Reminds me of Eve talking to the devil in the garden.

Lewis O`Conner was his name, A.K.A. "Mo Money"! And I mean baby boy kept money. He had the overflow. Even his mama had money. I think his whole family was rich.

After a few days of talking, we found that we only lived two streets over from one another. I was shocked to find that I lived in the same neighborhood as someone with all that money. (We *had* come up!) With a little persuasion, I decided one day to go home with him, just to see where he lived exactly, to bask in the lavishness of what I perceived his home would be like for a minute, talk, and maybe watch a little t.v. It must have been that darn scar on my brain that made me think that Mo Money would only want to talk. I hadn't figured out that Mo Money had something else on his mind though. Exactly why I couldn't figure that out after all the conversations about worms, I don't know. I guess maybe I was slow afterall.

I wasn't in his home long before I did catch on that Mo Money wanted to do more than just talk. Him kissing and touching on me as we lay in his bed gave it away. "Mo Money, I'm not ready for this yet", I told him hoping that there was a piece somewhere in his soul that would understand. But there wasn't. After whining a little and trying to persuade me that he was in love with me already didn't work, the real Mo Money made his appearance. He put down that whiny little voice of his and let the not so loving side of himself come out.

MO MONEY (MO PROBLEMS)

He reached into that cashmere coat pocket, you know the one that helped to draw me in in the first place, and pulled out a plastic bag filled with white powder. "What in the world does that boy have flour in his pocket for?", my dumb behind wondered. He put the bag of flour right up to his nose and took a couple of sniffs. "What is he doing?", I wondered. When he dropped the bag from his face, there was a totally different person in that room with me. Mo Money yanked his belt out of his pants and raised his arm as if he was going to whip me like I was his kid. My mind flashed back instantly to the beatings that I use to get from Betty. "Okay! Okay!" I said as I gave in to fear and sorrowfully allowed him to have his way. Now that he had physically penetrated my body, the door was open for mental penetration as well. He fixed it in his mind that I now belonged to him and he made sure that me and everyone else knew that I was his. He treated me like I was his property. It became a problem for me to even speak to my other schoolmates now.

One day, Mo Money and I were walking home from school and one of my friends spoke to me. There was nothing unusual about him speaking because we were friends and spoke to each other everyday. When I spoke back, Mo Money became furious. He was so furious that he grabbed me by my collar and threw me up against that big black fence right there on the corner of Dellwood and Watkins. You know that big fence that surrounded that little car shop on the corner; the fence with the sharp prongs on the top.

Now this intersection was an extremely busy intersection and was filled with a lot of my classmates walking home also, so there were a great deal of spectators. The same way that there had been when Killa took mama in the empty apartment and slapped her face. With my back against that fence, I fought him as hard as I could. I was finally tired of just letting people beat me and taking it. We brawled like two guys. Yea, he got his licks in but I got in some too. When it was over, the scars that were left on my shoulder where the top of the fence had pierced through my skin were deep and would take some time to heal. While I know that I didn't win the fight, you surely could tell that he himself had been in one.

I felt good after the fight. But that was the saddest part. Even more sad than the fight itself. The feeling that I had someone who was in love with me enough to hit me when he felt threatened by another man. I guess that by now I had developed the syndrome. 'I don't feel like he loves me unless he hits me'. Yea, my thought process actually took me there; so ladies I do understand that. But let me emphasize something right here. That is one lie straight from the pits of hell and it needs to be sent back from where it came. There are too many of us dying from the hands of our "lovers", and this vicious cycle needs to be stopped. Baby, if he's hitting on you, then he doesn't like you very much, never-the-less love you. Remember this, a person won't hurt what they love.

But I was like my mother now. I was sure enough somebody's woman.

I ran home all excited and couldn't wait to tell my mama that Mo Money and I had just got into a fight. I wanted her to know that I had found somebody that loved me like Paul had loved her. But instead of her celebrating my "entry into womanhood", as I called it, she scolded me and told me not to be involved with somebody who was going to hit me. She advised me if he hit me again to call the police. I wasn't trying to hear that though. I got so mad at her. Was she trying to get me to turn on the only person that I felt loved me? "But you let Paul hit on you all of those years you were with him", I thought. And besides, she didn't let the police whisk Frederick away for doing the things he had done to me. I wasn't going to whisk Mo Money away either. It seemed to me that now my own mama was jealous that I had somebody the way Frederick had been jealous before about Rowland when he caught us in the house together. I think that those two had some kind of plot to get me.

Little did I know that Mo money too had his own plot for me, other than just loving me. I didn't realize that his desire to explore further in the bedroom was preparing me for what he wanted in the end. He was already always pressing me to have sex whether I wanted to

MO MONEY (MO PROBLEMS)

or not, but I figured that to be my duty to the person that you love. But really you do understand that sometimes you just don't want to be bothered with that.

One day as he passionately kissed my body all over, I noticed that he was going down lower and lower. He went down past the points that were his norm. He went down low the same way that my cousin Ronnie had done. Before I knew it, sheer ecstasy. Yes, I once again was thrilled to have someone know about doing this to me. While it was definitely good, don't think that it didn't come with a price. When Mo Money tried shoving himself in my mouth I began to fight. "What are you doing?", I asked. "It's your turn now", he said. Well I wasn't going for that. He wasn't going to make me to be that kind of girl the way Paul had made mama be. I kept pushing him away and of course Mo Money didn't like being rejected. "I need to know you love me like I just showed you I love you." "But Mo Money, I'm not that kind of girl." All I could think about was him telling everybody at school what I had done to him. And you know the guys back then would talk about you some kind of bad for stuff like this. "So it's okay for me to show you love, but you can't show me none back." He sat up and started sniffing on that powder again. When I saw his eyes roll in the back of his head, I knew that I had better do something, and quick. I didn't want him to brand me with the end of that belt buckle the way daddy had branded mama with the hanger. It grieved my heart sorely but for my safety I officially became that kind of girl.

As time went on Mo Money began to do more things for me. My family was struggling financially now and sometimes we had nothing at all in the house to eat. He brought me food out of his mother's pots and started putting money in my pocket. He even bought some of my clothes that my mother could not afford. Mama cautioned me that I shouldn't accept these things from him. "When they start buying your clothes and giving you money they think they own you." She just don't know, he already pretty much owned me, but at least he loved me and I wasn't going to give him up.

Everyday at school was filled with some kind of drama with us. If

WHAT WAS MEANT FOR MY BAD...

I was caught speaking back to anybody that he didn't know or like, we fought. Not in private, but right there in the middle of the hallway. Everybody watching! If I was late making it to our locker between classes, I had to fight him. I had never had anybody to care about me or what I did as much as he did; in my whole life.

Although I was getting use to Mo Money's ways, I was still very much green to the lifestyle that he was trying to groom me for. I hadn't quite caught on that I was in the beginning stages of a pimp and hoe relationship. All I concentrated on was how good it felt belonging to somebody.

Then one day I saw him bickering in a corner at school with a girl that he had introduced to me as his cousin. When I thought about it, that wasn't the first time I'd seen those same two off in a corner alone. Then I started to see them more and more arguing and bickering. What would two cousins have to argue about so much? Then I started seeing him and Cherry.... fussing off in a corner. Now I know that she wasn't his cousin. Then there was a girl named Sherica. She didn't even attend Frayser school but she would walk up there it seemed just to argue with him when school was out. She was a bad girl that lived over off of Hollywood street and one of the ones that held that corner down on Shasta where Frederick's parents lived. When I say bad this time, I mean bad. She loved to fight. She was whipping people with iron poles and she always carried a switchblade. But none of us girls were a match for Mo Money. While Sherica was bad, he was flat out evil. They were exchanging words one day after school as I waited for him in the distance, (and yes, she new I was there waiting for him). I saw him hit her a couple of times in her face with his fist. She took those licks and then went on about her business and he and I walked home together like nothing had happened. I didn't ask him any questions and he didn't offer up any answers. While we were at his house, Sherica showed back up. She knocked on the door and when he looked outside and saw it was her, he instantly burst through the door and started running her head first into the side of his mother's brick house. He did this about three times. "My God, help

MO MONEY (MO PROBLEMS)

that girl", I prayed. I expected for her to collapse right there in the driveway and die from head trauma. Then his neighbors could hover over her body and say, "Damn, she dead". She didn't die though. She just left with a bloody, busted forehead. I felt so sorry for her but I was scared that he was coming after me next. But he didn't. He didn't do me as bad as I've seen him do to the others. On a separate occasion, I've seen him throw that same girl through his mama's glass table in the kitchen, shattering glass everywhere. I've seen him beat Cherry too. Now Cherry showed up to his house trying to get to me because the girls that I hung with at school had me picking with her while we were together in our little group. She came to catch me by myself without them to see if I wanted a piece of her then. You know that I didn't. It's foolish how we let others send us out to do things that we know we don't want to do. But anyway, Mo Money beat her down for me. I guess his rule was he could beat me but no one else could. Especially not another of his hoes.

My friends had tried to tell me that Mo Money had hoes everywhere but of course I couldn't see that. How could he possibly be a pimp and only in the tenth grade. That had to be some kind of serious demon. It was and he had me under his control.

One day Mo Money was absent from school. What a peaceful day it was for me, right. But as soon as school was out, he and Sherica were together on the campus. I knew that he was coming for me as we walked home together everyday. He wasn't going to miss out on checking on me, making sure I wasn't talking to anyone even if he had to bring his hoe with him. The two of them were arguing as usual. I thought to myself, "Both of them look mad and they bout to take it out on me." Sure enough, he started in on me about who knows what. I don't know who I had looked at that day, or who I spoke to that he didn't like. Maybe he was mad at somebody else, it didn't matter. If the next person had pissed him off, it was nothing for him to take it out on me or any of the others. Sherica was going to do what he told her to do because that was just the nature of this beast. If he would have told her to jump me, then she would have. Mo Money walked

WHAT WAS MEANT FOR MY BAD...

up on me fussing and pointing his finger in my face. With his raised hand prepared to hit me, Sherica pulled out her blade. "Dam", was all that I could get out. It was about to be head ramming time for me and this bitch is getting ready to cut my ass. As the tip of the blade swung open, imagine with me my surprise as she swung it around and landed it on his neck. "Now f___ with her if you want to", she said to him. Wow! She was actually taking up for me! Against him! Now this was the same girl who caught the city bus to Frayser just to beat Cherry, his other girl, with an iron pipe whenever she wanted. But my God! Something had caused her to have compassion concerning me. I guess Mo Money didn't feel like wrestling with both of us so he left and Sherica walked me home. She and I talked with each other for a little while in my mom's house. We were like friends for a brief moment in time. After that I don't really remember seeing her any more. Not to imply that something happened to her. She just didn't come around any more.

Mo Money undoubtedly was having someone outside of me encouraging him in the area of the bedroom. He grew more and more demanding with his sexual desires and requests. It was bad enough that I really wanted to stop having sex, especially now that I knew that he was with all of these girls, (but it was either ride or die...literally).

Okay. My time had come. I knew that I was on my way to death and hell when Mo Money's demon made him slip himself in my back side. Only he didn't slip. It was a process of aggravating and pain staking nudging and manipulation. I just knew that I was going to die. That was in deed the worse pain that I had experienced in my life. Far worse than any of his licks that I'd had to take in the past. Far worse than when my mother told me that I was lying on her husband. Far worse than anything that I could think of. Every muscle in my body became cramped and I would say that I believe that my heart stopped beating several times. He was too low down and evil to even try to lubricate anything to maybe help me a little. By the time he was through with me I was bleeding from everywhere. I had no control of my own body and so it too did what it wanted to.

MO MONEY (MO PROBLEMS)

Mo Money must have thought that he was in heaven but I wanted to tell him so badly that the devil wasn't getting into heaven. He liked it that way very much so of course what he liked he got, always. We continued our sex life that way and after the next few times I started to get use to it. As a matter of fact it eventually became *my* preference. He didn't have to ask me for it, I began to beg him to give it to me that way. I had become an addict. I was addicted to pain and abuse and it was impossible for me to distinguish what was love and what was not. Hell, I guess at this point in my life I had never experienced any love to compare anything else to.

The beatings from Mo Money increased but so did the sexual high after each. My body was filled with marks from the things he used to do to me. The deep bite wounds in my forearm finally healed and are invisible now. My jaw line fracture was blamed on an accident that had occurred during a game of basketball during P.E. It actually was the result of Mo Money's slap that was so hard that it left me unable to close my mouth for weeks. It eventually healed though. Through all of this, I still held on to the notion that he loved me and that I belonged to him.

The tenth grade year came and went and in the beginning of the eleventh grade I found out that I was pregnant. "Wow, me a mother", I said as I gazed at the doctor when he gave the report. But I was only sixteen. How could this be happening to me? Mama was pretty upset too. I could have sworn that I saw that woman put two cigarettes in her mouth at one time. "I told you didn't I. UhHuh! I told you", she said as she rocked back and forth on the chair in the examination room. But her words were swallowed by my own shock. She was so upset with me that she left me at the hospital alone for me to finish the examination and wait for the rest of the test results the doctors had performed.

I was sure the news about the baby would change Mo Money. And it did. He was ecstatic that he was going to be a father. He started doing my chores when he came over. He looked right funny in the kitchen washing dishes, but I thought we looked good together and we were about to be a real family now. At least I was safe from his poundings for the next nine months, after all you can't hit a pregnant lady, can you?

But the excitement about the new baby wore off of him in about a month or so. Whoever said you can't hit a pregnant lady lied. It seems that after the excitement wore off, Mo Money's fury came back worse than what it was at first. We were back to scrapping, but this time I was scrapping for two and I had to fight even harder to keep him from stomping my unborn baby right out of my stomach. I used the top of my head as a shield to protect her in my belly. I figured that if he knocked me unconscious and into a coma that the baby could still grow in my womb if that part was protected.

Any little thing seemed to tick him off. If he came to my house and I had my underwear on, we fought. He said that I knew that he was coming and yet I neglected to prepare for him. Up and down the hallways at school we still fought. The principal had to call the police on numerous occasions to get him off of me. This went on so much that Mo Money was eventually expelled from school indefinitely. But he was determined to let nothing stop him from getting to what was his (me and the baby). He started sneaking in the school when he knew that I would be changing classes to get to me. He caught me walking to my R.O.T.C. class which I had to get to by going outside. My instructor Major Routter confronted him when he saw him. The Major shoved me inside the brigade room and locked the door and all I heard was bodies being slung against the building. I don't know who was beating whom. I was so embarrassed that my teacher had to fight my boyfriend for my protection. "Mardyam, you have got to get away from that boy", he said to me afterwards. "He's alright, he just acts like that because he loves me", I said back. The look on Routter's face was one of sheer disappointment. I guess that I wasn't embarrassed enough at this point to walk away from all of this.

Well, I didn't walk away and Mo Money decided to finally show me how he got all of his money. He was a big dope boy. He began to bring his weed to my house for me to chop and bag it up for him to sell. I had never seen marijuana before in my life until then. He taught me how to roll the weed into a joint. We'd roll weed some, fight some about something senseless, have sex some, roll weed some, fight some, so on and so forth. He would smoke him a joint or two but never would let me have any. Mo Money has never ever allowed me to do any drugs with him. I got to watch him do it a lot, but it was a definite no no for me. Sherica and Cherry got high all the time and he didn't have a problem with that.

-6-

Who's Yo Daddy

DURING THE PREGNANCY I became ill and developed what physically looked like the mumps. I was about seven or eight months pregnant when my jaws and neck swelled to such a degree that the doctor's were perplexed. Although they were able to rule out the mumps, they still were never sure as to what it was.

The nurse at the hospital had my medical records pulled along with a copy of, apparently, my birth certificate. She was verifying my information. "Your mother's name is Annette Hardrick?", she asked. "Yes." "And your father's name is Samuel Halloway." "No!" I hurried up to correct her. "My daddy's name is Paul Jones". They obviously had the wrong medical chart. "Well it says here that your father is Samuel Halloway". "Well I guess they just made a mistake. I don't know anyone named Samuel Halloway," I said in my rebellious tone that I had developed by now. "Let me check on it", the nurse said. She left out of the room and my cousin that had brought me to the hospital and I really didn't think much of it. I just took it as the hospital had made a mistake somewhere that they would find and correct.

After we left the hospital and happy to know that I didn't have the munmps, my cousin took me home with her to my Aunt Freda's house. She called my auntie on the phone to let her know my results and jokingly told her that we had found out who my real daddy was. "By the way, we found out who Mardyam's real daddy is. Who was this Samuel Halloway", my cousin inquired. Suddenly and abruptly Freda said, "I gotta go. Bye!" She hung up the phone. "Well dang", we thought and the two of us just laughed it off.

Later on that evening when my mother made it in from work, I joked with her about it as well. As she walked down the hallway in our house and passed my bedroom, I yelled, "I found out who my real daddy is today". Now I couldn't see my mother from the hallway, but I could definitely hear her footsteps, and I definitely heard them when they stopped dead in their tracks. She turned around and came in my room. "Who?", she asked, as it appeared that she was playing along with me. "Samuel Halloway! Yeah you were tipping around on my daddy. Who is this Samuel Halloway dude", I jokingly asked . Little did I know that I was not prepared for the answer that I was about to receive. I was only joking. I knew who my daddy was, Paul Jones. He had been my daddy from the beginning. Before my mother could get another word out, Frederick piped in, "I told you that you should have told her a long time ago." "Are you mad at me", mother asked. "Mad at you for what?" It still had not sank into my heart what she was saying to me. I mean, I was hearing her words but I wasn't comprehending them. "I've wanted to tell you about your daddy but I was waiting for the right time. "This has all got to be a big joke. My entire life has got to be one big joke", I said to myself in a whisper as I stared in shock and disbelief. Okay, now I was mad. I was finally, finally mad. Everybody was a fake. Grandma Alice was no longer my grandma. My brothers, no longer my brothers. They were only halves. An entire slate of earth had just been snatched from under my feet while I was standing on it. You mean to tell me that I had put up with Paul's loud ass mouth, his abusive ass ways and was even willing to give myself to him to keep him calm and that man ain't even my daddy.

I was broken. I was broken to think that my mama didn't want me and now I find out my daddy evidently didn't want me either. I belonged to no one and the best thing that I did have was Mo Money.

-7-

The Birth Of Lujanette

I WAS AWAKENED early in the morning by my usual urge to pee. When I noticed that my panties were filled with blood, I knew that it was time. The baby was getting ready to come and I was anxious to meet her. I calmly went to my mother's room and woke her and Frederick and told them to get ready.

A short time after that, the contractions started. Light at first, but then hard enough to humble me to my knees a short while afterwards. Remember when I told you that I had become addicted to pain, I only thought that I had. Those contractions made me change my mind about how I felt about pain.

After we excitedly gathered my things and stopped by to get Mo Money and his grandma, we made our entrance into the Med. I relied with every fiber of my being on those doctors to get that baby out and deliver me from my pain. Not! You ladies who have had children know what happens to you if you're not dilated at least 3 centimeters right. You know it. I got sent back home. Not once that day, but twice. The doctor kept insisting that I walk. I tried to persuade him that it was dam hard for me to walk when I was down on my knees. He should have insisted that I pray while I was down there. Somebody help me, please! I think that on my third trip to the hospital, they went on and admitted me. Good, it's finally about to be over I thought.

THE BIRTH OF LUJANETTE

As I laid in that hospital bed hurting, I summoned God to come see about me. Mama and Mo Money were too busy arguing to concentrate on me. You see, they were only letting one person in the room with you back then, so Mo Money and mama had to take turns in my room. Can you believe that those two argued and bickered the whole time that I labored? Those two were clowning in the hallways at the hospital. Mo Money was mad when he had to come out to let my mother check on me. He threatened to leave the hospital and miss the birth of his child. My mother asked him how fast could he call his ride. Back and forth they went. All of this while I was hurting tremendously. So much back pressure. So much bed wetting.

Initially I tried to keep the two of them pacified but after a while I had to let them go and concentrate on myself and the baby. God was merciful enough to send his presence in the room to talk to me. The pain didn't go away but I had a chance to confess and repent of all my sins because I felt death was knocking at my door. For the next fourteen hours that I labored I held a one on one conversation with God. Mo Money petty ass had the nerve to tell me to keep my private part covered up because people were walking through the hallways and he didn't want anybody to see his stuff. "I don't care who sees it. They can send Willie the Whino in here for all I care. If he can take this baby out he can see all of the stuff he wants to see today", I told him. He acted like the fool that he was the whole fourteen hours that I was in labor.

Fourteen hours later, our baby was born. March 16th, 1987, a week and a half before my 17th birthday. Lunjanette Lashae Hardrick! I already had her name picked out. She didn't have to spend her first three days as girl Hardrick. She was a beautiful bird looking baby and Mo Money could not have been prouder. He used the hospital's phone to call my mother who was in the waiting room. "You are the grandmother of a healthy new baby girl", he said ecstatically. I'm told my mother even shouted for joy. Everybody just adored her as I ran down a few checks of my own on her. "Is she healthy? Can she see? Does she have all of her fingers and toes?" I asked all of the questions that I could think of. I actually was surprised to learn that she made it here healthy.

His entire immediate family showed up to the hospital to see Ms. Lunjanette. Both of his grandmas, his mother, his father, etc. For a little while, I actually believed that everything was going to be all right. That I would now have that loving family that I so desperately needed. But I would be proven wrong; again.

I came home a couple of days later and was as sore as I could be. While Mo Money was happy about his new baby, it was business as usual between he and I. The baby actually tore me when she came out so they had to stitch me up good. She was no more than four or five days old when Mo Money insisted that he had waited long enough for sex. He couldn't stand to just let me heal before he started ramming up in me again. I knew that I had to keep him satisfied because after all he was the only person that I had that cared anything about me. I couldn't risk loosing that. If I told you that anal sex hurt me the first few times, then I don't have the words to describe what I felt now. I had just delivered a baby for goodness sakes! My bed became saturated with blood. I could feel the stitches popping. The burning sensation would not cool. I couldn't; no I wouldn't cry though. He would probably get mad if I cried anyway.

You know, as I sit here and relive these events that took place in my life and as the tears roll down my face, I become angry with myself and ask how could I let these things go on. How could a person (me) be so weak minded and intimidated to put up with all of this? Then came revelation. The bible says, "For we wrestle not against flesh and blood, but against principalities, against powers, against the rulers of darkness of this world, against spiritual wickedness in high places" (Ephesians 6:12). I was infested with and under the rule and control of evil powers and demonic forces that had introduced themselves to me when I was but a baby. These forces had rooted themselves in my head and manifested themselves in the form of fear therefore, their wishes were my commands. Well, let me go on with my testimony because for all that I know there may be some of you

THE BIRTH OF LUJANETTE

going through these things right now. I know it looks bad right now but God does prevail.

After my six weeks were up, I went back to school. I didn't want to but mama insisted that I would get my high school diploma. Mo Money's grandma, Esther kept Lunjanette at her house which was, surprisingly, on Shasta street while I attended school. I would ride the school bus from Frayser to her house in the evenings and from there mama would stop on her way from work to pick us up and we'd go home. So it all worked out.

Now as I mention earlier, Mo Money was becoming increasingly demanding and bold as to what he wanted to do in the bedroom. One day he wanted to do it in his grandmother's bed, with her sitting in the living room where she could see directly into the bedroom. Did he want to do it where his grandma could watch us. "No Mo money", I said. "Come on baby, please". "Your grandma is sitting right there. She can see us you know". He got up out of the bed like he had really accepted and understood my 'no'. The next thing that I knew was I was being stomped on and dragged through the house by my hair and one arm. I felt my arm rip right from its socket. His sixty something year old grandmother jumped up to help me but he knocked her down flat out. He drug me through the front door and into the middle of Shasta Street. By this time a crowd had formed. I guess he wanted to make me a public example of what he did to his 'hoes' who got out of check. I couldn't control my bodily functions and urine just streamed down my legs. He stomped me until I was just a bloody pulp. I begged for someone to help me, but no one would. No one wanted to get in Mo Money's business just like they had not wanted to get in Killa's business.

Then finally, I knew it was about to be all over when he picked up that large concrete block. As he lifted that block over my head all I could think about was my little baby that was God only knows where during all of this. If I let him kill me, I would never see her again. As his arm was coming down to land the blow and before I knew it, the words were out of my mouth, "I love you". Now although I was looking him in the face, it would appear that I was talking to Mo Money. I wasn't talking to him though. I really was talking to God. I wanted Him to deliver me from my enemy's hand; again. As Mo Money's arm came down I didn't close my eyes nor cover my head. I was too exhausted to do so. Then, an answered prayer! I saw his arm with the heavy block in it jerk as if something counteracted his movement. Something had caught his arm in mid-air and spared my life. Whatever it was seemed to have spooked Mo Money because he took off like a flash of light down the street as if something was after him.

When I got up, there was blood and urine all over my clothes. My eye had already swollen shut from the blow it had suffered. One of the neighbors had my new baby and she was so upset that it took a while to calm her. I made a promise in my heart to her that from that day forward I would never let this happen again and that I would make life better for she and I. How would I know that I would later turn against her and do the same thing to her that was done to me under the control of the demonic forces deposited within me.

But I did manage to muster up enough sense after that to pretty much end things between Mo Money and I. I refused to let Lunjanette continue to go through that vicious cycle that I had gone through. We got a restraining order on him and had to go to court. Of course the judge ordered him to stay so many feet away from me.

Although ordered to stay away, he still was able to buy things for the baby. He just had to send it to the house by some one else. Oftentimes he would stand at the corner of my street and get one of my neighbors to deliver the pack of pampers he had bought to stay in compliance with the judge's orders.

The very last time that he came however, he wanted to talk to me about something concerning the baby. His mother brought him into our driveway which went against the orders the judge had set. He and I conversed for a brief moment before my mother came outside with a baseball bat and summonsed me to come inside. "If you don't get in this house right now girl, I'm going to beat you with this bat". "What did she say?", Mo Money asked. The two of them exchanged a few

THE BIRTH OF LUJANETTE

words and before I knew it he was in our house fighting my mother. I was still outside and didn't want to see what was going on inside. This was just all too much for me to handle. I didn't even want to be there. I ran next door to the neighbor's house and stayed. I could have done something to help my mother even if it was calling 911, but I really didn't care what happened to her at this point. I felt like she was getting what she deserved. You see, I guess that somewhere in here I had stopped loving my mother. Any way, all of the neighbors ran in and helped her.

Frederick was not at home at the time but when he found out what happened, he did absolutely nothing. He did not retaliate; just nothing. Wow, what a man who was in love with a woman!

With the family's minds focused on this new situation with Mo Money, there was a period of time that things were really calm. The home front wasn't nearly as stressful as before. But Frederick still had a few tricks up his sleeves that he hadn't yet used, and with some passing of time, he was back at it again.

One day after I had been home alone from school for quite some time, the attic door just came swinging down. "What the h...", I thought. Who was this in our attic? Had someone broken in and retreated there waiting for a good time to escape? Oh my God, it was Frederick! "How long have you been... Where is the car? What's going on?" I don't know where the car was this particular day, but there was no evidence at all of him being at home. He had been as quiet as a church mouse up there. What could he have possibly been doing in that attic all this time with the door closed besides sweating like a fool? Maybe he was using the attic the way that I had used the closet, looking for the 'presence'. He pulled this little attic stunt several times before I became aware of what was really going on.

One hot summer's day I was in my bedroom when a bumble bee flew in through a hole in the ceiling. He kept flying back and forth through the hole which caused me to believe that he was getting through to somewhere. Curiosity prompted me to stick a hanger in the hole to see if I could trace where the other end would show up.

◄ WHAT WAS MEANT FOR MY BAD...

Being that the attic was over my bedroom, you probably have it figured out by now. It stuck straight through to the attic. Had that bastard drilled or dug a hole so that he could peek in on me? That's why he was spending so much time in that attic. There was no telling what he had seen take place in my bedroom. There was no telling how long that hole had been there?

I knew for sure that I had to make a way of escape for my baby and I. I got my first job working at Dos Amigo's, a Mexican restaurant on Sycamore View and Summer. I went to school during the day and to work in the evenings. Although Mo Money and I was done with each other, I had become so use to the things that he did to me that I now carried them out on my own will. I became very promiscuous. I became involved sexually with my boss. The fact that there was about a 17-year difference between us didn't matter. On the nights that I had to catch a ride home with him, we would make a pit stop somewhere. Sometimes that was at his house. Sometimes it might have been on the side of the road. Wherever and however he wanted me, he had me. The funny thing about it all was even though I was about 17 years younger, I taught him a lot. You should have seen the look on his face when I told him that he could have it in the front sometimes but that I wanted it up the back most of the times. But what really got him was when I told him that I wanted him to hit me. Yes, I told him to hit me. That was the only way that I would get the most pleasure out of the experience. He was real unsure about that at first, but he eventually caved in to the idea. Whenever he was not available to take me home, he had another guy from the job to take me. Of course he had already told him that I would take care of him on the way and I did just that. I allowed my boss to pimp me out to other people on the job.

Since Mo Money was no longer around at school, I was free to date and see whomever I wanted to, and boy did I. I became the bad seed at school. I cut classes any time I felt like it. I would walk in through the front door and straight out through the back door. It was nothing for me to verbally disrespect my teachers. Everyday when the

THE BIRTH OF LUJANETTE

principal made the announcement over the intercom, "do not admit to class, Mardyam Hardrick...." My name seemed to have been the first name he called. That meant that I had to go to the office to see why I was in trouble and couldn't go to class.

By now I was jumping into bed with whomever I wanted to whenever I wanted to. When my graduation from high school day came, I walked across the stage with yet another baby in my belly.

"Snap out of it Mardyam", I said to myself. "You can't stay around here and keep getting pregnant laying up on welfare. You've got to do better than this." I determined in my heart that I would leave Memphis and never come back. It was then that I understood the desperation that my mother must have felt when she wanted to abort me. Like me, she already had one baby at home; but unlike me, she didn't have the funds to get the abortion, I did.

I shortly signed up to go into the Unites States Navy. I figured that I would be safe there. The government would be taking care of me now and I was sure that Uncle Sam would do a better job than what my natural family had done.

My recruiter spent a lot of time with me preparing me for entry and yes, of course, I was eventually in bed with him also. He was an older man and the only thing that really impressed me about him was that 'clip' on his hip. He wore a .45 caliber pistol that seemed to turn me on in every way. That .45 called my name seductively especially when it opened itself up to me and showed me all the power that it contained inside. Fourteen golden nuggets on a clip and one in the chamber at all times waiting for anybody to get out of pocket. I fell in love with it and longed to have it make love to me. I envisioned all of that power up in me. My recruiter complied with my wishes. I made him use that thing in a way that it was definitely not created to be used. All the devil had to do to take me on out was cause the safety to slip and all of my female parts would have been all over the room. It is with reluctance that I even share this part with you, but my point is that these types of desires and fantasies are real. People experiment with them all of the time. I can recall an actual incident that was reported on the news where a preacher put his pistol up in his wife and it went off and killed her. Now if the people that's teaching God's ways to mankind are struggling with such demonic control, then how much more would the people who don't know God's ways at all struggle. It's up to people who have been delivered, to pray for, teach, and live exemplary lives for those who remain under such control.

Now the recruiter had a soft heart and he began to have strong feelings for me. He absolutely loved the 'fun girl' that he had run across. But I knew that I had to leave it alone when he started talking about leaving his wife. I wasn't about to break up a marriage nor have a serious relationship with a man twice my age. I was too young and too hot for that. I told him that I didn't want to see him any more until it was time for me to leave.

The time did finally come for me to leave and the morning that he showed up at my door was filled with sadness. It was about 2:00 am and Lunjanette was still sleeping. It hurt my heart to have to sneak out on her this way but I wouldn't be able to stand watching that little face as I said good-bye. I loved her so much, but I had to go away to make a better life for us as I had promised.

-8-

Leaving Memphis

IT WAS BOTH exciting and a relief to me to be on that big Delta Airplane. I had never been on a plane before. I had a window seat and I planned to look out of it as we transited Memphis' city limits. The cabin was a close knitted space and we were all like many members enclosed in one body sharing one common goal, getting to our destination safely. Whites, Blacks, young, old, people in business suits and people in sweat suits comprised the passengers' list on this somber morning. We stayed hooked up to the terminal for a while so the Memphis Blues still haunted my soul for an additional hour or so. But as soon as that door was closed and that little truck pushed Mr. Delta back, I felt freedom rise in my veins. Bye Frederick, bye Mo Money, bye mama and bye my little baby. I was not coming back, EVER. That Delta plane hit that runway faster than Paul could have ever thought about driving his thunder car. It ascended to the sky in a slope and carried me far away from all my enemies in the bluff city.

After about four hours of being up in the friendly skies, I touched down in Orlando, Florida. This place would be my new home for about the next eight weeks. It was late when all of us new recruits were finished getting processed in. The coolness of the night air coupled with the tons of paperwork that we had to complete caused us to become exhausted and we longed for sleep. We got our orders,

WHAT WAS MEANT FOR MY BAD...

"Shower up and hit the racks." There were about twenty of us and we had a total of thirty minutes to get everybody showered and in the bed. We filled the open shower stall like crabs in a pressure cooker. The stall provided absolutely no privacy. Everybody and everything was out in the open. I was surrounded by naked women everywhere and had to fight hard to keep those wrong desires from surfacing. The 'don't ask don't tell' policy would keep me covered throughout my new career.

It seemed as though I had just laid down when all of a sudden I was awakened by what sounded like bombs exploding in the barracks. "We can't be at war already." No, it actually was the sound of metal garbage cans being thrown against the walls and onto the floors by people who came off as savage beasts. "Get up you pieces of shit." It couldn't have been any more than 3:00 in the morning and I know that I had just closed my eyes. We all had just been introduced to our new mama and daddy for the next eight weeks of our lives and they had been given governmental permission to treat us real bad. "Eight weeks of this kind of treatment", I thought. I couldn't help but to wonder if I could make it.

We spent our days exercising and marching in formations, sweating and passing out on the grinders. The grinder was just a big open concrete lot behind the barracks that had no shade for safety, no benches nor grass for sitting, no fountains for drinking, just no comfort at all. It was like the desert except instead of sand there was concrete.

I had God's favor on me in bootcamp though, and since I had His favor, I had the favor of my Company Commander (CC) as well. Everywhere that we went, we had to march to a cadence that ended up being called by me. "Left, left, left right left", was all that I had at first. After I got a little good at it I was able to add some rhythm and slang with it. "Left two three foewa, two three foeeeleft two three foewa, left righta layeft." I was again bad with that marching and cadence calling.

According to regulations, I was too tall to be the company's guide-on. That's the person who carries the company's flag and gives the signals to execute different moves while in marching formation. That person had to be shorter so that everyone all the way in the back could actually see the flag that they held. Of course my CC ignored that regulation and made the guide-on as well as the cadence caller. She would always shout at the other girls to, "March like Hardrick." When we weren't in formation and was allowed to have leisure time to shoot the breeze, they would tell her "We can't march like Hardrick." I had those hips working.

During our graduation ceremony we had what we call a 'pass-in review.' That's when all of the companies that were in training, male and female companies alike, had a chance to show off their marching skills to top officials. We were all paraded around to be looked at and were actually judged in different categories. The CC's were judged on how well their company was trained. The guide-ons were judged on how well they handled their flags. There were many other categories that were judged as well. When we marched in front of the judging officials, we were to do an 'eyes right.' That meant to turn our heads towards them and give them a hand salute to show them honor. I mean we had to execute this with such precision that we looked like one person doing it. We had to make it look sharp. My job was to extend my flag pole horizontally to display my company's identity. Upon the command 'eyes right', I extended that pole, executed a sharp right head turn looking those military officials square in the eyes. As they nodded their heads in approval of my style, I slipped them a wink of my eye to show my appreciation and led my company forward. We of course came in first place for having the best guide-on on the compound.

After the graduation ceremony I looked around and saw that everybody was visiting with their families. There were proud mothers and fathers everywhere. Some people even had cousins to show up. People had traveled from far away places to be a part of and to witness this momentous occasion on behalf of their loved ones. I looked around some more and realized that there was no one there for me.

◄ WHAT WAS MEANT FOR MY BAD...

That was all right though. I don't know why I had even expected someone to show up for me.

Later on after all the excitement wore down, we were allowed to go out on the base. I went to the club and found myself not having such a good time. Something was wrong. Anytime that I'm around music and not having a good time dancing, something just ain't right. Maybe it wasn't all right that I had no one to show up for the graduation. "Girl you know that don't nobody want you." The thoughts in my head started telling me that a lot.

It just so happened that the CC that had been in charge of one of the male companies in the group was in the club. I only knew of him from seeing him parading around with his company out on the grinders. He remembered me from carrying the flag. I didn't know his name and he didn't know mine, but he did know that I wasn't having a good time at the club. After a few questions from him he asked if I wanted to go to a house party with him. He snuck me off base and took me to the party as his guest. By the time the night was over, he was another man that I could add to my list.

After my eight weeks of bootcamp I got ordered to go to the Naval Operating Base (NOB) in Norfolk, Virginia. My first duty station was a ship, The USS L.Y.Spear (AS-36) a submarine tender.

I arrived on the dock about 7:00pm on my first night. My heart sank when I caught sight of that huge mass of steel pasted against the night's black sky and docked along that little pier. I was sure that the homemade looking ladder that I had to climb to board the ship would fall right into the Atlantic Ocean when I made it half way up it. "Request permission to come aboard", I sounded off like I had been trained as I saluted the ensign (American flag) and the Officer of the Deck. "Permission granted", he responded. As I handed him my orders so that he could check me into my new home for the next four years, he and his messenger responded "deck ape." I couldn't help but to wonder what he had meant by calling me a deck ape.

They made a phone call to have someone to come and escort me down to where I needed to be. I was all right up until that point. Even with being called a deck ape and not knowing what it meant. Then I got a scare that made me long to be back home in Memphis and possibly understand the meaning of deck ape. J.C. was her name. I quickly got the feel of the real United States Navy upon her arrival and presentation of herself to me. J.C.'s skin was as black as that same night sky that the ship was pasted against and that now surrounded her. She blended in with the darkness so well that I could hardly see her. But what I could see was her bulged out eyeballs and teeth that showed white as snow. This sista was wearing Navy dress blues (which were actually black in color) with pants way too short. She had the nerve to have on white baseball socks. You know the kind with the two blue rings around the top. Oh my God! The deck ape!

She escorted me down below decks to our berthing area. This is the place where we actually lived and slept. My bed was one of three thin metal slates that were all welded to a metal wall. The metal walls were stood back to back with three bunks on this side of it and three on the other side. The berthing compartment itself held about 45 bunks like this. All of the bunks held a thin mattress on top and the tops of the bottom and middle ones could open and be propped up like the hood of a car, exposing different sized compartments to house your belongings. The top bunk had the luxury of having two large standup lockers for your possessions. My CC had already warned us against bringing a lot of clothes because there was simply not enough room for it on a ship, and she didn't lie. "Go ahead and change into your civilian clothes and I'll take you up stairs to get you something to eat", J.C. said. "But I don't have any civilian clothes", I said to her back. "What", as she looked at the other ladies that were in the room. "This bitch didn't bring no civilian clothes. What the hell is wrong with you?" That, ladies and gentlemen, was my introduction to the real United States Navy. I quickly fell into a state of depression behind that and wanted to call and beg my mother to come and get me. But since I couldn't and it was the weekend, I just crawled in my bed and slept until Monday morning.

That following week, I began to go out on the town with J.C. She

◂ WHAT WAS MEANT FOR MY BAD...

actually became a real good friend to me and because she had an apartment I had somewhere to go when I wanted off of the ship. I started mingling with the other girls too. They took me to the club on base and you know that I fit right in. The bass from the club's speakers penetrated my very soul. I closed my eyes and got lost in the music. I remember dancing to Lisa Stanfield's "I been around the world and I can't find my baby. I don't know when I don't know why, why he's gone away and I don't know where he can be. But I'm gonna find him." I was a natural. Every man in the club wanted to dance with me. My energy was high. Then the D.J. mixed in "It's electric…" I did the electric slide through the whole club. I got the crowd pumped. The D.J. made me promise that I would keep coming, and I did.

-9-

Doing Me

AFTER I GOT comfortable in my new habitat, I began to indulge in my sexual habits again. I quickly built a reputation for myself that seemed to have differed in points of views taken from the males vs. the females. The males saw me as a very fun and satisfying in every way companion while the women saw me just as a pure slut. It didn't matter to me what the women thought though. I figured that I was a woman who just lived out the fantasies that most women wish they had the guts to. By now, I had learned to substitute love with sex and needed to have plenty of sex so that I would think that I was getting plenty of love.

I made up in my mind that I would build a business using sex. I wanted to be a call girl and start my own escort service. Nothing trashy though. I pictured myself in a long black evening gown. Pearls draped around my neck and dangling from my ears. My hair eloquently pulled up in a bun.

I sometimes pictured myself as a phenomenal stripper, so wherever there was a party, I was sure to be the entertainment. (Somewhere in this world, there are homemade centerfold pictures of me pretty much in the nude, I'm sure on somebody's wall.)

I had become feisty and could get the boys to do whatever I wanted them to do, even take a picture with nine other guys all on their knees with me standing over them like I was their sex master. I had all of that power and it seemed to have brought so much pleasure to so many.

Then one day I ran across somebody that made me bring all of that fun to a halt. He wasn't going to stand for me sharing myself with other people nor running my soon to be "world famous" escort service. I complied with his wishes because really in the final analysis what I really wanted was someone to care enough about me to say, "Mardyam, Stop!" More than having all of this bad fame, I just wanted somebody to love me. You see, that's really what we're all looking for as we jump out of bed with this one and that one. We just want to be loved.

His last name was Weatherby (in the military, we called each other by our last names). He was one of my supervisors in the department that I worked. We kept our relationship on the down low in the beginning to keep everybody out of our business. Weatherby had a best friend named Bobbie Davis. He too was one of the supervisors that I worked under. One day during an inspection, Petty Officer Davis and I had an altercation. He was scolding me for not having a ballcap with the ship's logo on it. That was a part of our uniform that identified what ship we belonged to. Several other supervisors had already made that clear to me and when he said it, that feistiness took over and I let him have it. "Seaman Hardrick, you need to get a ballcap with the ship's logo on it", he said to me. "I will when I get paid," I shouted back. "Are you trying to tell me that you don't have any money. Now I know that's a lie. You just left bootcamp and you couldn't spend no money there." "How in the hell are you going to tell me what I got", I responded back while in ranks; everybody listening. Any body who has been in the military knows that you don't get smart with your supervisor, especially while in ranks. That's a definite reason for disciplinary action. "If I said I ain't got no money, then that's what I mean and you ain't gonna make me have any. I'll get a ballcap when I get paid like I said". Ohh Petty Officer Davis got so mad at me. I had showed him up in front of all of the other recruits and he wanted to get me badly. "Make sure you all assign Seaman

Hardrick to work for me today. I got her", he said to the supervisor in charge of giving the job assignments.

Well, he got me. Working for him that is. I was assigned to him and he had determined that he would work me extra hard for my smart comments. We conversed the entire time that he stood over me driving me like a slave master; but before the end of the work day I had him sharing my work load. You see, conversation is what got Eve messed up in the garden. You have to be real careful with whom you're holding conversations because smooth talkers will talk you right out of your destiny.

It was something about my attitude that he liked and when he found out that I was from Memphis he claimed me as his home girl. He was from Jackson, Mississippi, which was about two hours away from Memphis. I guess that did pretty much make us home boy and home girl in that big navy world.

He became interested and started trying to talk to me but I had put that lifestyle on hold because of Weatherby. "Petty Officer Davis, I don't mess around with married men", I told him. I truly had broken myself from that after my recruiter started talking about leaving his wife to be with me. A lot of things I was but I would be no homewrecker.

Weatherby was from Mississippi as well so the two of them had already bonded long before I arrived. One night after we got off from work I went to Weatherby's house with him to just kick it like boyfriends and girlfriends do. We had been sitting around for a little bit when there was a knock on the door. It was Davis. Weatherby cracked the door so Davis could not see inside. Like I said, we were dating on the down low. But Davis pushed the door opened determined to find out what was up inside. He made his way in. He was stunned when he saw me. "Ohh, you got Hardrick up in here", he said. "I was on my way some where else and just thought that I would stop by here before I went there. And look who you got up in here!" Now Davis was a drinker and he beckoned for Weatherby to pour us all just one drink before he left. I wasn't a drinker and didn't care much for alcohol but I took a drink with them anyhow. You see, conversation will make you do things that you normally wouldn't do. We started drinking and I got relaxed and stretched out in the middle of the floor. Weatherby came and laid down beside me. Before I knew it, Davis was down there too. Both of them started kissing on my neck. I didn't like where this was going. I was about to get got, again! I started fighting, trying to get them off. They held me down though. I did not want this to be happening especially with this married man. And plus there were two of them and one of me. I was about to have a train ran on me and I didn't like that idea at all. Could it be that I had been set up. My hopes of giving up that bad lifestyle was fading fast. I threatened to tell what they were doing when I made it back to the ship if they carried it any further. Davis stopped for a brief moment to console me and promise me that we were just going to have a little fun. He vowed that no one would know what went on but us. He gave me a few more sips of alcohol and then I did what I had learned to do before. I let them have their way. We went into the bedroom and I'll let you use your vivid imagination to finish this scene.

Now Weatherby had a roommate that I knew absolutely nothing about. When I heard the front door open, I wondered who it could have been. "That's just my roommate", Weatherby said. "Roommate! What roommate?" I asked. By that time I saw somebody peek into the bedroom I guess to see what all the commotion was in there. When he figured out what was going on I heard him say, "Shoot, let me get in on this". I ended up in the bed with three men at one time. My mental state was like one that was on drugs. I had plenty of strength and actually the three of them together was still no match for me.

After I came to myself the next day, I was angry because I knew that any chances of Weatherby loving me had now certainly been blown. No man will love a woman who has slept with him and his best friends. Needing someone to blame I reported what they had done to me to our department head when I got back to work. What did I really want from the lieutenant? How could I really expect for him to do anything at all, after all I was a whore and I'm sure that he knew of my reputation. Still, for some reason a part of me was disappointed when he scolded us all and said that he never wanted to hear about the situation again; from no one (Shhh, don't tell nobody). What had happened was pretty much swept under the rug. That further confirmed for me that that was just the way life was. Especially for a woman like me. You take it and you go on.

After that incident, I conceded and Weatherby, Davis and I made up and became like partners in crime. We partied together and three way sex was a constant with us. Whenever Weatherby and I went to a hotel room, Davis was there. All three of us were like "And the three shall become one flesh". This phrase that I just made up is a perfect example of how the devil is always twisting up the words of God. The word of God says, "And the two shall become one flesh". I was in pure sin and if God had seen fit to take me from this world at this time, I would have lifted up my eyes in hell.

As time passed on, Davis decided that he wanted to have just one night alone with me, without Weatherby. I wasn't sold on that idea much because I really didn't want to make Weatherby any angrier than what he might have already been. I was also still determined not to involve myself emotionally with this married man. Everyday at work, I had to hear Davis talk about how much better he could perform if he got me alone. Day after day I had to listen to how he could satisfy me better than Weatherby.

Finally I gave in to him. "Just one time", I told him, "And keep it between me and you." This time I was the one saying Shh, don't tell nobody. We went out alone, first to the club. We actually had lots of fun. Davis loved to dance just as much as I did, where Weatherby was sort of a wall flower. We left the club and went on to the room.

As soon as I made it to work the next morning I was confronted by Weatherby. "So you and Davis doing yall own thang now, right?" "What the…what the…", I was lost for words. How did he find out? Of course there was only one way he could have known. And no, it wasn't God talking through the preacher this time. Davis had betrayed me. Weatherby was very angry and would have nothing else to do with me. The two of them even exchanged a few words but decided that it wasn't worth loosing friendship over a whore. Ouch!

Remember that first night that Davis stopped by Weatherby's house and said that he was on his way somewhere else, well he was going to see his 'girlfriend' that night. Yeah, that man already had a girlfriend on the ship but I didn't know it. He cut her visit short to indulge in that three-some (well four-some) we had and when she found out that he had been neglecting her because of me, she was furious. It didn't matter to me that he had a girlfriend though because I wasn't going to continue to be with him anyway. It really wasn't supposed to have been about he and I in the first place. Plus, I will still testify that I felt guilty that I was messing around with a married man. I think I had guilt about that because of a conversation that Frederick and I had years prior when I was a little girl. We were listening to the radio in the car and that song "As we lay" by Shirley Murdock came on. I told him that I didn't like that song because of the part when she said, "You're leaving me. I know you've got to hurry home and face your wife. I would never want to hurt her no. She would never understand. You belonged to me for just one night as we slept the night away. As we lay." He commented to me "baby you will understand it one day when you become a woman." "No I won't", I angrily yelled back at him. I didn't want to understand anything that he understood. But anyway, I heard that Davis's little girlfriend asked him "Why are you messing around with that baby. What can that baby do for you?" (I was only 18.) She had asked the absolute wrong question about the absolute right person. Even though I was in a world of sin too, it was hard for me to understand how two married people could become angry about what the person that they were cheating with did. Both of them were married. What were these people's problems? Now I had to show this hussy what this eighteen year old baby could do for that thirty-one year old man. I had a score to settle and so I had to pour it on a little more.

I had to blow his mind for sure now. I started dressing very provocatively in the sexiest teddies that were made. It was nothing for me to go out on the town with Davis in a black lace and leather teddy with the drawstrings on the side as my blouse.

I no longer limited sex to just hotel rooms with him. If he wanted to slip into an empty space on the ship during the busiest hours of the workday, I made sure that I was available for that.

Because I was living on the ship and had no bills, my money stacked up nicely. The government was already sending Lunjanette a check once a month so I didn't have to send any money home. It was nothing for him to get in on the ship the next morning and find a three piece suit with a matching "big daddy's" hat laid out on his rack, accented with a teddy bear and a card of love. (Yeah, I knew how to play the game.)

Whenever he had duty, meaning he had to spend 24 hours on the ship to watch over it, and had to stand watch from midnight until 4 am, I would set my alarm clock just to call him. I would call him about 1,1:30 in the morning while he was standing on the quarter-deck of the ship on patrol just to have phone sex with him. I would tell him how much I was thinking about him at that time. He would almost be ready to abandon his post to get down there in that rack with me. When we went out at night I would make him pull the car over and let me out. With the headlights beaming on me I would dance for him and all of the passing cars right there on the highway. He loved when I serenaded him with Keith Sweat's 'Make it Last Forever' or Baby Face's 'Whip Appeal'. Mind blowing is just what I was naturally. Anyway you get the point. And then I ordered him to drop his little girlfriend. He shouldn't have been cheating on his wife anyway. But guess what. By this time, I had invested too much into this relationship just to call it quits.

There came a weekend when Bobbie hosted a divisional party at his house. Everybody from our division was invited, including me. Now keep in mind that he lived with his family out in town. I had much respect for that and had no intentions of acting a fool in their home. I would be on my best behavior. I promise!

I showed up, of course, with some of the other people from our

WHAT WAS MEANT FOR MY BAD...

department. I could tell that Davis was on pins and needles. I played it super cool though. I made it appear to his wife that I was dating one of the other guys that were there, so she wasn't worried about anything. She assumed that I was with a guy named Chris. I partied like we always did out in the clubs. But this time I was drinking on my own free will. I think that I had drank a little bit too much as Chris and I slow danced all night long. I became so intoxicated that I could hardly stand. I didn't pay any attention to Chris getting too close and feeling me up while we danced. In his defense though, He probably was truly trying to hold me up. Davis noticed though and he didn't like it one bit. Every move that I made, he was eyeballing me. He became angry as I acted like I didn't care that he was watching me. My whole point was that he was at his house with his wife throwing a party. He eventually got mad enough to tell one of the other guys to get me the hell up out of his house. "Now how that fool gonna get jealous at a party that he and his wife were hosting because I'm trying my best not to make her suspicious of the two of us. "That fool done lost his mind", I stuttered to one of my friends. "Don't worry, I'll get my own self out of his dam house." And I left walking, headed back to the base. Not before kicking all of the tail lights out of that brown New Yorker of theirs though. I heard that I left his wife running around trying to figure out who had done it, but I was already gone and my buddies at the party were not telling. Everybody was hush hush, (shhh…don't tell).

I was so drunk that I was walking out in front of cars about to get hit. I remember them honking their horns at me. Then a friendly ride pulled up next to me. "Girl, get in this car. You're too drunk to be out here walking." It was Weatherby. Boy was I glad to see him. I would be safe now. Little did I know that he had another agenda in mind. Instead of taking me to the ship, he took me to a hotel. "I'll get you a room for the night", he said, so you can sleep this stuff off. We went in the room together and got in the bed. That was all right with me. Of course I passed out and slept the night away. I woke up to devastation and surprise finding four other guys in the room instead of Weatherby.

He was no where to be found. That dog had set me up, again. But they say payback *is* a mutha. I only knew one of the guys that were there; Brown. I have no idea who the other three were neither where they came from even to this day.

I was mad as hell and was about to call the police. When Brown saw me upset, he began to apologize and help me gather my belongings. The other guys ran to keep from getting a rape charge. "I'm sorry Mardyam, but Weatherby called us and said that you would love to have all four of us together. He said that you were into that sort of thing." I guess that's the price that I had to pay for what I had done.

Davis was mad too. He confronted Brown and demanded that he told him who the other guys were. Brown didn't even know who they were. They were friends of Weatherby. Davis and Weatherby got into an actual fight this time. Davis seemed to have cared for me a great deal at this point. With his help I picked myself up from that situation and just went on. I seemed to have found somebody that was with me through thick and thin and that became priceless to me.

By now though, hatred and bitterness began to fill me. I found myself hating my mother. I hated her more than I even hated Frederick, her husband. Somehow all of this was her fault. My whole life was her fault. This same woman that I had loved so dearly as a kid; yes the same woman that I once stood guard over, I now hated. It was her fault that I had to be here in the first place. Would it had been good for that turpentine and those pills to wipe me out??

Anyway, Because Davis cared for me deeply, it became easy for me to unleash my anger on him. He became my sounding board. My anger literally turned into fits of rage against him. Tension between us grew as I now demanded that he leave his wife.

I remember one day I could not get in touch with him. He must have been with his wife. I became so angry that I turned on myself. I snatched all of my jewelry from my ears, neck and fingers and threw it into the Atlantic Ocean from aboard the ship. I had always purchased the finest of everything, jewelry included. I pulled off all of my rings including one that my mother had bought me for my thirteenth

◄ WHAT WAS MEANT FOR MY BAD...

birthday and threw them overboard. I snatched the necklaces off of my neck and threw them overboard. My diamond stud earrings, over the side. When Bobbie did show up, I pulled a pair of scissors out on him and threatened to stab him with them. I had developed a very destructive nature and more than Davis would be affected by it.

-10-

Meeting Daddy Samuel

THE GUILT THAT mama had about me not knowing my father must have prompted her to try to find him. She found out that the last known place he lived was Santa Barbara, California. She made a few phone calls and was eventually connected to him.

I was surprised when Samuel and I were actually speaking on the phone for the very first time ever in my whole life. I really had my own biological father and I was happy about it. As it turned out, he had known about me this entire time. He even visited me when I was about 9 months old. Mama says he invited us to move to California with him. He and his wife were separated and going through a divorce at that time. (Wow, I didn't think that he knew I existed.)

He too had been in the military. He told me that I had a brother that was serving time overseas. How ironic is that? All three of us had military service running through our veins. He contacted his son, Ricky, introduced us to each other and we chatted on the three way as often as we could.

Samuel and I decided that it was time for us to meet each other, so we made plans to come to Memphis. I carefully planned my military leave to make sure that I had enough time to spend with my father. This was actually about to happen. I was about to meet the other person that I belonged to. I flew home on the first flight that I could get headed to Memphis. I must admit that I was a little nervous. I hoped

◄ WHAT WAS MEANT FOR MY BAD...

that I would not be a disappointment to him.

I had given him the number so that when he came in town he could contact me. I waited for his call. And waited. And waited some more. A no call no show. That's what he was. My father actually had the audacity not to show up. What a devastating blow for a young woman who had already suffered so much abuse and neglect. Boy didn't God pick out a family for me. "That's okay", I had to tell myself. "It wasn't like he had been a vital part of my life any way". I just hardened my heart and decided to forget about him. I finished my vacation and got back to Virginia.

A couple of weeks later I received a phone call. It was Samuel. "What happened to you", I asked him in an angry and disappointing tone. He went on to explain that he did not want to show up without having told me that he was in a wheel chair. He was a paraplegic, paralyzed from the waist down. He didn't want me to be disappointed seeing him for the first time that way. I made myself understand. After all, I had worried about being a disappointment to him, and my reason for worrying was not nearly as severe as his cause for concern. I assured him that the only thing that was important to me was having my father and I gave him a second chance. Some time down the road we had planned to meet again. My Navy Chief was gracious enough to let me go back on military leave again.

As I packed the morning of my departure I got a phone call. It was my father's girlfriend. She was calling with some unbelievable news. "I was calling to let you know that your father just committed suicide. He shot himself in the head." That fucking bastard! How dare he do this to me! Selfishness consumed every part of my being. It was over! I would never get to meet my father. EVER! My own father hated me so much that he would rather die than to be in my life. That proved it. I was nothing and wasn't deserving of anyone's love. Life had played another cruel joke on me and there was absolutely nothing funny about it.

I did everything that I could to try to erase any memories that I had of him. I tore up all of his pictures that he had sent to me. I burned the newspaper article that praised him for starting an organization for handicapped people. I wanted no memories at all.

I went on to Memphis anyhow only to learn that my brothers' daddy Paul had died a couple of days after Samuel. God had taken both of my daddies at the same time. Was it something that I did? Both funerals were held while I was in Memphis and the anger that I had would not allow me to attend either of them. "To hell with them both". I heard that Paul's children actually argued whether or not my name should be on his obituary. Do you honestly think that I gave a dam if it was or not. That meant absolutely nothing to me. I went back to Virginia and determined to close the door on Memphis forever.

-11-

Right Choice Wrong Time

ABOUT FOUR MORE years passed and Davis persuaded me that I needed to go and get my daughter and raise her myself. Ohh I really was not prepared to make that move. I figured to leave well enough alone. I trusted that she was being taken care of and that was good enough for me. I tried not to imagine that perhaps she was suffering the same fate that I had suffered at the hands of Frederick. Is he tickling her too?

Besides that, my own baby no longer had a bond with me. I know this because she had become violently sick a few years earlier. The doctors called me home because they actually thought that she wouldn't make it. It was very hurtful to find that the only person's arms that gave her comfort during her battle were my mother's. Now, while she knew me as her mother, she no longer knew me as her nurturer. Why would I take her from the people that she loved?

I listened to Davis and decided to go through with the move. The time came and we drove to Memphis to get my little darling. The scene was a very sad one. My mother was crying because she was loosing Lunjanette and Lunjanette was crying because she was leaving mother. I wanted to cry but had to play big girl in front of my mother. No way would I let he see me weak.

My baby cried the entire road trip to Virginia. That feeling of rejection that I first felt from my mother rose within my spirit and I begged Bobbie to turn that car around and take her back. I became angry at her just like I was angry with every one else.

Bobbie was trying to make me do the right thing but it was at the wrong time. I had so many emotional scars that I actually lacked the skill of knowing how to truly love, even my own child. I was a horrible, horrible mother. I had made up in my mind that I would build her tough. I would make her so hard that no one would do the things to her that they did to me and get away with it.

My bootcamp tactics set in and I was very abusive to her. It was nothing for me to whip her and throw her little body against the wall when she made me angry. I threatened to throw her through the window the same way the "black widow" had threatened me when I was in bootcamp. When she came in from school, she had to stand at attention at my front door and request permission to go to her room and wait for me to respond. Sometimes I responded and sometimes I didn't. ("God bless her soul and protect her from this fool.")

Bobbie was a big shield for my baby. He knew my mind state and acted as her protector. He spent time with her and took her places with him where there were other children for her to play with. He tried to keep her away from me as much as possible.

I grew so cold that I became known to Bobbie and his friends as the Black Apache. Whenever his friends wanted him to go out, they would tell him, "ask the Black Apache can you hang with the fellows tonight."

My physical body soon lined up with my stone heart. I experienced so much tension in my neck that from behind my earlobe on down to my shoulder blade felt like there was a balled fist underneath my skin continuously.

Now while Bobbie was good for my baby, things between he and I changed. Actually, I was the one who changed. With the purchase of our new house and the promotion I had just received in the military, I knew that we could not continue to party the way we did in the past. We were acquiring more responsibilities now. But Bobbie was a drinker. He loved music and just couldn't stay out of the clubs. I

◂ WHAT WAS MEANT FOR MY BAD...

found myself pulling away from him and started to realize that the sin I had committed was coming back to haunt me.

I started going to church a lot just to be away from it all. I now was at church as much as I had been in the clubs earlier. I didn't see church as place that I wanted to be with my entire family. We had two services on Sundays and while I didn't mind taking my baby to the first service, that 6:00 pm service belonged to me. I didn't want to have to be bothered with anyone. See, church was all that I had that was mine alone. I could close my eyes, cry, think, pray, beg God, whatever I needed to do to release the tension. I didn't want to have to answer the 50 million questions about why I was crying that your babies ask when they see you hurting.

I found myself beginning to sink into depression. My military career became the highlight of my life and when the work day was done I didn't want to return home. Davis and I had been together for about six years by now and I had never cheated but suddenly I found myself in need of someone to talk to. The pull to fill the empty void that I had inside my soul prompted me to enter into a relationship with someone else (Sounds familiar). It's so ironic that over all of these years of having sex with Bobbie that I never got pregnant, but the first time that I messed up with that other person I was impregnated instantly. Oh my God! There's nothing like having to go back through calendars trying to line up that last period with the last time you had sex with the person you're with versus the first time you had sex with the new person. I was on pins and needles waiting for that doctor to tell me how far along I was. "Mrs. Hardrick, you are about nine weeks pregnant", the doctor said. "Great", I thought. "That means that the baby is Bobbie's". My next trip to the doctor I was informed that they might have been a couple of weeks off. It was a possibility that I wasn't as far along as they had initially told me. This was not good news. At least my mama knew who her baby's daddy was. The baby (me) just didn't know.

When I told the other guy that I had been seeing the news, he was happy at the possibility that we might have a baby together. He wanted to have a part in the baby's life if it was his and he even asked me to marry him. I couldn't do that. Even though I was miserable at home, I had made a life with Bobbie and I couldn't just walk out. The other guy informed me that if the baby was born with sickle cell trait, then it was his.

I understood again how mama felt when she got pregnant with me. This was a bad situation and I didn't think that it would be good to keep the baby. I contemplated having an abortion but God pricked my heart and said, "No, not this one."

I decided to keep the baby, but something in me would not let me carry the baby to term without Bobbie knowing the truth, however. I went to my pastor while at Mt. Sinai Church in Porthsmouth, Va., and told him what I had done and that I wanted to tell Bobbie the truth. He set up a meeting for us and was instrumental in cooling an otherwise hot situation. Tears streamed down both of our faces as Pastor talked to us about forgiveness. He reminded Bobbie that he cheated on his wife to be with me. Now he had a decision to make. Would he forgive me or would he leave?

-12-

The First Marriage

BOBBIE DIDN'T LEAVE and we got married on March 29, 1994, the day after my 24th birthday. My new name was now Mardyam Davis. Damion Lequan Davis was born on the 27th of July that same year. Of course he was born two weeks later than the original due date that the doctor had given me; and of course he was born with sickle cell trait. Now I hadn't told Davis about the blood disorder that I was warned about, so as far as he was concerned the baby was his.

As time moved on, I slipped deeper and deeper into depression and became withdrawn from my family. I still carried that destructive behavior and in my rages would tear up things in the house. All of a sudden I would just start breaking up dishes and anything else that got in my way.

Often times Bobbie would call my mama to try to get her to calm me down but that just made it worse. I had grown to hate her and there was nothing that she could say that I would listen to, even if it was right. Most of the times I didn't go to the phone when she was on it. I just laid it down.

One Wednesday night, Davis decided that he would go to church with me to try to smooth things out at home. "Oh No! the devil is a liar." I did not want to take him to church with me but what would I tell the church folk, "My husband wanted to come to church with me

THE FIRST MARRIAGE

but I wouldn't let him." That just seemed to have gone against all of the rules.

We went to church and of course Bobbie was drunk. I sat with my head hung all night. The Pastor was speaking on the effects of secular music on us. When he said something about Aretha Franklin's music, Bobbie blurted out in slurred speech, "I don't agree with that." The congregation could tell that I was embarrassed, but Pastor Sessoms humbly responded to me, "It's all right sister."

After service Pastor told to me to bring him back. "We are going to work with him and get him saved", he said. "No!" I thought. "How could they do this to me. I don't want him here with me. I don't care if he gets saved or die and go to hell. Can't he go to another church?"

Bobbie did come back, again and again. He started getting involved with the men of the church and then, one Sunday, came the ultimate betrayal. He joined my church. The entire church cried out with joy as he walked to the front. "Look at him standing up there infringing on the only sane part of my life that existed.", was all that I could think. Then the evangelist came and escorted me to the front to stand beside him. I wanted to swing on that bitch so badly, right there at the alter. It took every disciplined skill that I owned to keep from hitting her and walking out right through the front door.

Deeper and deeper I spiraled and I grew to hate having sex, but I still slept with him because, as he often reminded me, the Bible said that I could not withhold from my husband. Every time that he touched me I felt that I was being raped all over again. The tears would stream down my face as he did his business. When he was finished, I would go crawl into the bed with my son to try to find sanctity and cry myself to sleep.

My mind had started to drift from me and I knew it. I began to imagine that I was that eight year old little girl again and that God had placed a protective bubble around me. No one could get in it to harm me. I saw myself as a child happily playing on a playground running through the wildflowers on a bright sunny day from the swing set to

WHAT WAS MEANT FOR MY BAD...

the merry-go-round. I was the only one there and I had all of God's love and protection for myself.

I adopted a survival technique for myself. When I felt myself loosing it, I would yell out "duck". That was to let God know that I was about to go through and I wanted Him to fight the battle for me. I was going to duck so that I would be out of His way when He swung at the enemy.

My mind was tired and I couldn't take life any more. One day I took a butcher's knife and decided to cut my throat to end this torture. I remember falling back against the kitchen wall with the knife to my neck asking God why had He allowed me to suffer this and if I died would he let me come to heaven. All I heard God say was "hold on daughter." "What am I holding on to?" I cried. Then He went away.

At church the following Sunday, I listened to the words that the Praise and Worship Team sang, "This is your day, this is your day. Bring your burdens to the alter and Jesus will wash them white." I made up in my mind that when I went to the alter this time, that I was not going to leave the same way that I went up there. When Pastor made the alter call, I waltzed right up there in front of the line. I was desperate for healing. When he came and laid hands on me, I grabbed him with a firm grip and I wasn't letting go until I was changed. The armor bearers ran up to pull me off but I was determined, like Jacob in the bible that I wasn't going to let go until he blessed me. Boy was I mad when they peeled me off. I needed to have an encounter with God and the carnal minds of the leaders in the church would not let me. So I returned home even more depressed than I was before I left.

It had been a couple of years now and regrettably I was pregnant again. This time I was sure that Bobbie was the father. But at this point I could not do another baby. I didn't want to be pregnant and I flat out didn't want this baby at all. I had already decided against having another abortion since I was into church and all now, so I went to the Lord in prayer again. "God, this is Mardyam again. I've messed up again and I really, really can't do this. Now I don't want to have an

THE FIRST MARRIAGE

abortion so the only way that this can end is if you take this little baby to heaven with you."

During this time we were friends with another married couple, Barbara and Mike. They had tried to have babies several times before but the babies were all born too early and died. Barbara was pregnant again too and she had already started having the same complications that she always had. It didn't look good again.

One day while we were at work, she and I ended up in the restroom together. I said "let me pray for your baby." I prayed and asked God to give the life that was inside of me to her. This was her fourth time and she really wanted her baby. "Lord, I'm not trying to be evil about this situation but my life is too heavy for me to bear this. What could I ask better for a friend than to sacrifice this life so that hers may live? If I've asked amiss God please forgive me and help me."

A couple of days later a gentleman stopped in for a haircut at the school where I taught on base. I was a Barber Instructor at Fleet Training Center, Norfolk. I actually taught the classroom portion and let my students who already knew how to cut hair teach the hands on portion of the class. Some kind of way we were holding a conversation about my pregnancy. I remember that I told the man I didn't want to be pregnant. He kept asking me if I was sure that I didn't want the baby. There was absolutely no debate in my mind about this one. I reassured him that I didn't. He said okay as if he had something to do with giving me what I wanted. He got his hair cut and went about his business. "What a strange conversation for me to have had with somebody that I don't know", I thought.

The morning of my next doctor's appointment came. As I prepared myself I felt in my spirit that this would be the morning that the doctor's tell me that my baby wasn't alive. I was having my first ultrasound so Davis decided to go with me.

We made it to the doctor's office and the nurse started with the ultrasound. After a few strokes across my belly, she called for a couple of more doctors to come in the room. I knew then what was going on. They took over the ultrasound procedure and after repositioning the scope several times they knew the verdict. They didn't tell me themselves however. "Mrs. Davis, we're going to send you to a specialist to let him take a look. There's no cause for alarm right now. Sometimes our equipment can't pick up things so early in the pregnancy," they said. "What a great lie," I thought. "I already know that the baby was dead."

We made it to the specialist and he performed yet another ultrasound. "I'm sorry Mrs. Davis. The baby does not have a heartbeat" he reported. "Are you saying that the baby didn't make it?" I played dumb. "No ma'am. I'm sorry, your baby didn't make it." Bobbie took the news kind of hard and was sad in his heart but in mine there was rejoicing. I know that sounds cruel but that was my state of mind then.

My friend Barbara still went through her pregnancy with complications, but in the end she gave birth to a big healthy baby boy. They said that I would forever be his Godmother no matter where this navy life leads us. Somewhere in this world I have a God son named Nevin.

I figured that I had suffered being in a marriage that I was so unhappy in long enough and began to ask God's forgiveness for destroying Bobbie's first family. "God I repent for hurting his wife and his children. If you could see fit to bring his family back together again to sort of right the wrong that I did I promise that I will step out of the way and let them mend things." Bobbie and I eventually divorced and he went back to his first wife.

In the mean time, I still struggled with being a good mother. I provided well the physical things that my children needed. My career was very successful and we were quite comfortable financially.

I would buy groceries but I wouldn't cook them. I knew my children had to fend for themselves so I had an opening cut in my cabinets to allow the microwave oven to be lowered so that they could cook their own food. Lunjanette was about 9 and Damion was about 2.

It was nothing for me not to see any parts of my house except my bedroom for weeks at a time. When I got them from the baby sitter's house, I came through the front door walked straight into my bedroom and closed the door on my children everyday. When they knocked on the door, I just hollered "leave me alone" and I pulled the covers over my head. Lunjanette was a good girl. She found them something to eat everyday and cooked it in the microwave. She took care of her little brother. One day Damion tried to make himself a hot dog in the microwave and burned it to a black crisp. (I just wrote about that to try to lift my spirits as I write about how awful I was.)

One day while Lunjanette was at school she and her teacher got into a casual conversation about eating dinner with family. Lunjanette made mentioned that I didn't cook for them. When her teacher asked how did she and her little brother get food to eat, she told her teacher that she did the cooking.

Now during this same period, Lunjanette suffered from bad toothaches. Often when she was at school she would complain about the pain. She never mentioned to the teacher however that she was already being seen by a dentist so it appeared as though I was neglecting this issue too.

Letter in the mail! Mardyam Davis versus the Department of Children Services. "This letter serves to inform you that you are being investigated for child neglect" it read. It went on to state the reasons for the investigation listing chronic health problems with my daughter as the main reason. Well, that part was covered. All I had to do was take her medical records to the school to prove that she was under the care of a dentist. I did and they dropped the case, for a minute any way.

Some time later, Lunjanette was jumping in my bed when she slipped hitting her face. The fall put a crook in her nose and it actually looked as though it was broken. She went to school as usual and the teacher asked her what happened to her nose. Lunjanette was afraid to tell her what she had done. I guess because she thought that she would get into trouble for jumping in the bed. When she did tell the truth the teacher assumed that she had made it up because of her hesitance to tell her initially and I was accused of breaking her nose.

◄ WHAT WAS MEANT FOR MY BAD...

Letter in the mail! Mardyam Davis versus the Department of Children Services. "This letter serves to inform you that you are being investigated for child abuse" it read. This time they actually had to come to the house to see the conditions in which we lived. That's where they messed up at.

My house was phat for a young girl. When you pulled up in front, you were greeted by two towering brick flower beds one of which held the imbedded mailbox. The lights that were atop the beds screamed nothing but class and at night gave a warm welcome to the guests of my neighbors in the Green Run community. I'm sure that the burgundy New Yorker that was trimmed in gold was backed into my driveway first and that my Lexus finished it off. When you entered my home, you entered into a mirrored foyer graced with a grandfather's clock that chimed every fifteen minutes and piped out the exact number of dongs every hour for each hour of the day that it was. My living room was dressed with a wood burner that was surrounded by red brick. My son's keyboard outlined the black and gold mini bar that sat in a section of the room. My dining room held its table that seated eight and stayed fully dressed with each plate setting, ready to serve. The soft light from the matching hutch lavishly showed off my crystal pieces that had been carefully selected by myself. The French doors that separated my kitchen and den from the dining and living rooms were stained cherrywood on one side, to match the color of my dining ensemble, and an off white on the other side to enhance my beige and off white kitchen cabinets. My den, which shared an open space with my kitchen, had a full-blown fireplace and the burgundy leather couches carefully matched the burgundy that I had dressed the children's glass 4-seat dinette table with in the kitchen. The cream-colored ceramic floor tiles throughout the main thoroughfares gave a hint of just the right amount of rose color to accentuate every room in the house. My children both had their own rooms and every luxury such as cablevision came with it. Their bathroom was affixed in the hallway while I had my own private bath in my room. There was enough food in the refrigerator to feed everybody on the block and, thanks to my mother coming in town to help, there were pots of cooked food covering the top of the stove.

When the social worker inspected our living conditions he was in awe. "There is no way that your children are being neglected," he said. "Case dismissed." I was glad to have the victory but there's a point that can be made here. People get so caught up on what they can see with their natural eyes that they become blinded to the truth. Yes, my children and I had great material things, but on the inside we were suffering immensely. The glitter and glamour of things possibly kept us from getting the help that we so badly needed.

-13-

Returning To Memphis

I HAD WARRED in my mind long enough and I told God that I would go ahead and give in to insanity. I looked at myself in the mirror and saw all of the beautiful hair that graced my head. It was thick, long and full. People were always asking me if it was all my real hair, which it was. I saw it as a gift from God and since I was so angry with him at this time, I took a razor and shaved every piece from my head. When I say that I shaved my head I mean that the back of my hand had more hair on it than my head. My children came in from school and all they could do was stare. My son thought that it was funny though as he laughed and exclaimed, "Mommy you look like a man".

When mama got word of what I had done, her parental instincts kicked in and she made her way again to Virginia, this time to bring us back to Memphis for good. I was returned back to the exact same family, the exact same house and had to sleep in the exact same room that I had said good-bye to eleven years prior and swore that I would never return.

I had to start over from the beginning again. I had to live as an adult with the man who had molested me all of those years when I was a child, and with the mother who had turned on me for him. Humbly I walked around there and acted as if nothing had ever happened, offering up the respect due to a mother and father but who deserved it not. Sitting at the dining room table with the person that helped to almost destroy me and to break bread with him as if there was pure love abiding took great discipline. But as I think about it even as I write this, maybe God was throwing me back in his face so that he could see that he had not destroyed me. Could it have been that the demon inside of him trembled while he looked upon me as we broke that bread because his plan to kill me had not prospered. While it's true that I had suffered some injury, he had not made me his own personal sex slave like he thought that he was going to nor had God allowed me to kill myself behind his antics like he thought that I would.

I absolutely dreaded the thought that I would one day be like my mother as I watched her parade around submitting to the desires of that man. I decided not to become involved in a relationship ever again. I became very content with just going to work every day and coming home to a challenging crossword puzzle to finish before I put my kids and myself down for the night. It was that kind of thinking (not wanting to subject myself to a man) that opened the door for that homosexual demon to rise yet again. Although it had lied dormant for years it was not dead and I began feeding it with my thought process. I reasoned with myself that maybe it wasn't relationships that were a problem, maybe it was just relationships with men.

I found myself being drawn to the strip clubs late at night trying to find a new "kind" of someone to be with. I frequented the Pure Passion club for gentlemen just as much as any man would have. I always found myself hoping that I would not ever run across my brothers while I was in the place.

When I entered into the foyer of the club, I could physically feel the demons go into my body with a force so strong that my very arms and legs got heavy suddenly. I was so anxious to get on the other side of those double doors that served as a barrier to all of the action as security patted me down and when I did, I willingly gave my mind to the master of the house (Satan) and my money did follow. I even had a particular girl that I went there to see and whatever she wanted she got. Money was no object just as long as I could get that quick fix that I needed.

I eventually met a young lady (not in the club though) and we began bonding. I was surprised when I found out that she was a musician at one of the most prominent churches here in Memphis. She ushered in the presence of God before His people through her music. She sat under the powerful anointing preaching of the number one leading Bishop of Memphis, Sunday after Sunday and yet had this terrible yoke of bondage around her neck. We both did.

I found myself having compassion for her. I'm not talking about the lustful sex passion that I wanted from her, but I felt a desire to see her get free from her bondage. I could see her wounds and I wanted nothing but healing for her. God started messing with my heart and right in the middle of a supposedly intimate evening, I just started ministering to her, not out of my own will though. Somehow the script got flipped. I emphasized to her that she was a beautiful woman and that God had made her specifically for a man. I told her that she needed to wait on God to send her a Godly husband just like I needed to wait for my husband. I left her. As cruel as this may sound, I had nothing else for her. The word was given and the door was closed. I never saw her again after that. The desire to minister to hurting women rose within me, but I knew that I wasn't yet ready to serve in that capacity. I still had wounds and still battled with desires that would kill any chance of a ministry before it even got started.

-14-

Another Marriage

TAKING MY OWN advice, I decided to give another relationship with a man a chance. Although Ali was quite different from anything that I had been used to, I managed to convince myself that heaven had sent him along the way just for me. You see, I had heard that Muslim men were obligated to take excellent care of their wives and families; and I didn't mind cashing in on that. After all, that's what I figured I needed by now: somebody to take care of me. I was finally going to get my rest through this man.

More than having him to take care of me though, I was ever so fascinated about his attire. He wore a long dress and little beenie on his head. "A man in a dress!" How peculiar was that? I could really make a statement to the world with him by my side. Something like, "My man owns oil, or at least a couple of beauty supply stores. What does your man own?" That's what he looked like. You know those Muslims be having they own stuff. But seriously, The proper name for what he wore is "jabeel", but my point is that I liked it, a lot! It seemed to have excited that rebellious part of my being and was going to let me say, screw this Memphis ghetto living. I was about to be shown a different kind of life. Was I about to have to wrap my head and face too?

But when I found out that he had just finished serving ten years in prison for murdering someone when he was only sixteen, I went over the top. You see, he wasn't a foreigner born and raised of the Islamic faith. He was straight out of Dixie Holmes and had found his religion while incarcerated. But still I found myself having an even deeper attraction to him because he was "gangsta", "and a Muslim,(Osama Bin Laden around here). I was happy to know that he was a man well capable of protecting his family if need be, especially me. He was definitely no punk. At the same time I thought that he would be so grateful to be free that he would do all that he could to hold on to a family (to hold on to me).

He had swelled visions and actually did own one store down in Sanatobia, Mississippi already. He talked about being the leader of nations. He was going to be the king of the Underground Negro and I was going to be the queen. He was going to make it and I was caught up in the sound of it all.

Disappointment came however when he told me that he had a wife. "A wife!" I shouted in disbelief. I still wasn't down for messing around with a married man again. Then he explained that in his religion he was allowed to have more than one wife. "I don't believe you", I said. "You mean to tell me that the woman you got at home will be all right with you seeing me." "Yes, and if you don't believe me, we can call her right now and get this straight," he responded. We did call her and she was all right with it and I tripped out. Then I reasoned with myself and said, "I might as well since men are going to cheat any way. This way I won't consider him cheating". We could both have our cakes and eat them too. As it turned out though, they had not taken a legal vow of marriage. They had gone before the Muslim minister, the Imam, and announced their marriage. While this was legit in his religion, it held no weight in America. So really, as far as I was concerned, he just had a girlfriend. I figured that she was a sister who was just as frustrated with life as I was and decided to just settle for whatever.

He tried to be as fair as he could with both of us. He alternated his days between she and I. He spent one day with her and the next day with me. The golden rule was that he was supposed to have provided equally for the both of us. He could do no more for one than he did for the other. Sometimes he would take us out together and the three of us would do fun things like play laser tag and then have dinner. Bro had it going on.

Ali and I were able to talk about all things. He became my very best friend and I learned to respect him very much only after one month or so. His motivational speeches of how we were going to conquer the world put me in the mindset of Bonnie and Clyde. We meditated a lot on our dreams and goals. It was nothing to find us walking around the track at Ed Rice Community Center at 9:00 at night.

After about two months, he and I were married, legally. I needed him to prove to me that he really loved me by signing marriage papers and making me his legal wife. I didn't want to just be a girlfriend. I know that you all are shaking your heads and going "two months! That was stupid!" That's good if you are. That means that you know better already. We hadn't known each other long enough to know if we would really *like* one another, nevertheless love each other. That man signing that marriage certificate didn't prove that he loved me at all and I was too selfish to consider what us getting married would do to that other woman. Hell, we were at his family's BBQ and his uncle was a licensed preacher. With BBQ sauce on his fingers, he just simply signed the marriage certificate and so did we. There's love for ya!

On the night that we got married, Ali had a surprise for me. We rented a hotel room on Elvis Presley Blvd. You know the purpose that hotels over there serve, right (for the prostitutes and pimps). What a wedding extravaganza! It was late and I had just showered and was stretched across the bed relaxing and realized that I had forgotten my lotion in the car. I sent Ali out to get it and had to wonder what was taking him so long to come back in with it. Where had he gone? Eventually, I heard the door open. Without ever looking up I felt the palm of a hand filled with lotion run up the back of my leg. "This is not Ali," I thought. As I turned to see who it was I was stunned to see a woman in the room holding my lotion. " Your husband told me you

WHAT WAS MEANT FOR MY BAD...

left your lotion in the car." Oh my God! The boy had hooked me up. Moments later he came walking through the door. He had hired a prostitute to spend our first night of marriage with. I must say that I was pleased with the idea. She began to do what he had paid her to do but something wasn't right. I could tell that she really didn't want to be doing what she was doing. She seemed to have been uncomfortable with his every touch. Had she too been a victim of some sort of sex crime? Nine times out of ten she probably had. What had she gone through that would convince her to sell her body on the mean streets of Memphis?

Out of obligation to the same struggle that I assumed she and I shared, I made him leave her alone. Conversation ensued between she and I. I said, "Sweetheart, you don't have to do this if you don't want to." Then she exclaimed, "But he has already paid me." "I don't care about the money that he already gave you. Why are you out here doing this?" "I don't know. I really don't like what I'm doing." "You don't have to do what you don't want to do. Put your clothes on and get up out of here." Then that same little girl prostitute looked at me as she took her turn to speak as if in a position of authority for a brief moment and said, "This is not who God called you to be. Why are *you* doing this?" I was caught off guard and virtually speechless, as I did not expect this to come from a prostitute. She got dressed, headed for the door and proceeded out, turned around as though she had forgotten something valuable and returned only to kiss me on my cheek as a daughter would kiss a mother.

I knew that God was trying to tell me something but for some reason I wasn't getting it. So as time passed I started wondering if maybe I had it all wrong like Ali said I had. I was no longer sure if God was speaking to me through Christianity. There seemed to have been a lot of loop holes in it for me thus far. I decided to denounce Christianity as my religion. I still believed that there was a Supreme being out there and became willing to try my husband's religion to try to connect with it. I asked him questions and he taught me as we curled up with the Koran at night. I had to change the type of groceries that

ANOTHER MARRIAGE

I brought into the house. Of course you know that there could be no pork at all, since the beginning. I started eating lamb and whatever other kind of meat that they sold at the Mediterranean store on Highland street. I think that the meat that they sold had to be cured and cut a certain way. Anyway, I was willing to submit myself except for one thing, I just couldn't bring myself to cover my hair and face. My hair was my glory and my face, beautiful. I just wasn't ready to give that up yet. But maybe with a little bit more time and a little bit more understanding of the religion I would eventually submit even the very hair on my head.

The only thing that a little bit more time brought about was Ali's impatience with his store to turn a profit and the emergence of his Dixie Holmes up bringing. He had been about his hustle when he was but a young boy running the streets in the hood, in and out of Tall Trees Correctional Facility for youths convicted of burglary, auto thefts, selling dope and later even murder at the tender age of sixteen. With a straight ten years of his life dedicated to the system and after about only eight months of freedom, he got about his hustle again. He soon forgot about his alternating days between she and I and the streets started to get more nights with him than either of us. Now you know that it's hard to deal with one unhappy woman at home, now imagine having to deal with two.

Things were falling apart and I managed to rattle his nerve so much that my own husband searched for someone else to pawn me off on. One day I got in the car on the passenger's side as he was about to drive me to work. I saw a key chain that had a picture of a young lady enclosed in it. "So she's the reason why you've been hanging out late at night." "Mardyam don't start. See you always got come with that dumb stuff." One thing that I can say about Ali is that I've never heard him cuss. "That's for you", he continued. "What do you think about her?" Of course me with my old profane mind was down for it. Later that night I trailed him to the girl's house. He didn't even get out of the car that he was in. He just showed me her apartment and drove off. He was in a hurry trying to get to that dam studio where he was recording some music. When I finally made it home in the wee hours of the morning, I was comforted to find him home and up waiting for me; after all, he was still my best friend.

I watched as the streets slowly pulled him back to them more and more and it seemed as if he wanted me to go with him. Evidence that he was dealing drugs again started to pile up. One evening while I was a student at the local community college I realized, as I pulled off campus, that the tire had gone flat. I came to a stop on a side road that paralleled the school. A friend that I was dropping off and I popped the trunk to see if there was a spare tire and were surprisingly greeted by a revolver just lying there. He hadn't tried to hide it the least bit. If I had still been on school campus and popped that trunk in front of the security guard, I would have been immediately arrested.

Once again on a separate occasion, I made a trip to McDonald's for a simple hamburger meal. I was digging in the door panel for the few pennies that I owed the cashier. I noticed about five or six little balls of what looked like the silver chewing gum wrapper from doublemint gum. It was clear that there was something in it because it was hard and had a definite shape to it. "What in the world is this", I asked his mother who was with me. "Let me see that daughter", she said sort of in a hurried voice. "Well I'll be… that's a rock!" "A what", I asked her. Could it be that my best friend and husband let me drive my car around with crack cocain right there at my fingertips, at the cops fingertips and really at his mothers fingertips because she was an addict and she stuck those rocks right in her pocket and took care of that when we got home. Boy was he angry when I told him that his mother had got him. She was living with us at the time and I had to beg mercy from him to stop him from throwing that woman out in the cold. Drug dealers don't play about their shit.

Ali finally got caught up out there in those streets. He had left home and I very rarely saw him. I didn't know where he was staying nor how he was eating. Before I knew it I was receiving a phone call from one of his buddies. "You know they got your boy", the voice on the other end of the phone was saying. "The police picked him up about 4:30", he said. He passed all of the necessary information to me so that I could go see about him and of course I was there to see him on the very next visitation day, as any good wife would have been. I was glad to know that the police had transported him safely to jail. I had been so afraid that I would have been getting a phone call saying that Ali had been killed. Ali had told me before that he wasn't going back to jail, so I worried that it would be death.

How sad it was to see my husband transform before my very eyes from the man in the "dress", to the man in the depressing county orange jump suit. I was so green about this kind of life that I didn't even know how to get him to hear me through that thick glass that you can see each other through. I was talking loud enough to interrupt everybody else's visit with their loved ones. He had to tell me to pick the phone up to talk to him. How pitiful! I didn't belong to this lifestyle.

I was determined not to give up on my husband. Even though he had eight years of parole time to back up if he violated, he assured me that the most that they were going to make him do was one year. I could hold out that one year.

They moved him from 201 Poplar to a Facility in Henning, Tn., which was about an hour and a half away, but I still desired to make it to his visitation every weekend. During the course of his previous cross-country drive as he tried to 'find' himself, he had burned the engine up in the Lexus so the car that we had now was rolling only on a wing and a prayer. I wasn't ever sure if I would make it to Henning, but I headed out anyway. You see, that's the kind of girl that I was, loyal. Sure enough one Saturday the car broke down on one of the back streets on the way to the jailhouse. This back street seemed to have had miles of nothing but trees and winding roads. Anybody could have stopped and did anything that they wanted to do to me once they realized that I was stranded and alone. Oh but somebody did stop. It was about three or four of them. It was a team of Godly men coming from Bellevue Baptist Church out of Memphis, Tn. on their way to do prison ministry in Henning. (You know, that's the church with the three big crosses that can be seen from the express way

WHAT WAS MEANT FOR MY BAD...

when you're going towards Appling Road.) They were kind enough to give me a lift to the prison. I left my car on the side of the road and finished my journey to the prison with them. As they went to minister to the inmates they assured me that they would wait for me after visitation and get me back home. I spent time with my husband as they did what God had called them to do. They then saw me safely to Millington, Tn., which was only about 20 minutes from my front door and where my brother was waiting for me when they dropped me off. "God please bless those men at Bellevue Baptist Church and their prison ministry. May their ministry have an effect on a life behind bars just as much as or more than it had on a life that was free".

Ali was always trying to make something happen. Even while he was in jail he was thinking of ways to make money. He started back up with the leather good products. He was making leather belts, wallets, Bible covers, etc. Often times he would send finished products that people had ordered from him to me and I would have to get it to the people and collect the money. That was cool because that was an honest living.

One time I had to go and pick up a package for him and deliver it to a third party that would be waiting for me on the compounds of the prison. I figured that it would be either some money or some tools to complete a leather job. When I arrived to the spot where I was to pick up the package, I was a little unnerved. He had sent me to a store in a rather rough area of town. I had to give a code word just to get to see the guy that was giving me the materials. I didn't feel safe at all. I got the little brown box that was handed to me and got back to Frayser as fast as I could. There was something that drew my curiosity to that little brown box. I wanted to know what was in it. What would I be transporting up the highway and right up to the front door of the prison? I tore into the box in front of my cousin who was unfortunately addicted to drugs at this time. A box full of heroin! I couldn't believe that my husband wanted me to bring drugs on the prison's campus and pass them to some Muslim women who would take them further inside. My cousin broke down everything to me about what was in the box. He told me the kind, the grade, what people did with it, everything. I was so furious. Now I know that the smart thing to do was not to transport the stuff. I was so afraid, however, that the man that looked like "scarface", the man that gave me the box, would have Ali killed in jail and come after his family also if those drugs did not make it. I felt that I had to get this package there at least this one time for the safety of my family.

Do you want to know who I called on to help me make it through this? It wasn't Allah nor the prophet Mohammed. I called on the name of Jesus. I called on the One who had been there all along to see me through all of the mess that Satan took me through. I said "Jesus, if you see fit to let this thing come to pass, allow this to be done and behind me, I promise that I won't get myself caught up like this any more." I had to go back and pick up the One that I had laid down when I doubted his existence. Have you ever found yourself saying, "God if you just get me out of this one….." I know you have. Then I heard the Lord when he said to me "Girl, choose you this day whom you will serve", and I cried unto the Lord, "As for me and my house Lord, we will serve you" (Joshua 24:15). It was over for Ali and I. I didn't want to be a drug dealer nor the messenger.

I was in the maize of life desperately trying to find my way out. Although I still knocked on a couple of wrong doors while feeling my way, I knew that I was finally moving in the right direction. There would yet be a couple of more stumbling blocks before I would finally break the barrier to peace of mind and joy unspeakable.

-15-

The Final Straw

<u>THE FINAL STRAW that broke me on down</u>. After leaving Ali and being by myself for about a year, I found myself again giving relationships another chance. No, this man wasn't a drug dealer. He didn't even drink nor did he smoke. He didn't beat me nor did he require any perverse sexual acts of me. And because he didn't, my twisted mind actually wondered if there was something wrong with *him*, especially when I dipped back and tried to engage him in my world of strip clubs and threesomes and he didn't bite. "What gives?", I wondered. Of course I had to ask the question, "Are you on the DL? Are you gay?"

    This man went to work everyday to a job that paid him six figures and was an excellent provider for the daughter that I eventually gave him. Heck, he had already proven to be an excellent provider for the other three of mine that I had before his baby even came along. It's rare to find a man that's willing to take super care of his own children, nevertheless children that's not even his. Seems that there could not have been a better man for me (or any other woman as far as that goes).

    But there were still problems and the biggest problem was me. I had so much that was damaged in me that no matter how good he tried to be I would make something wrong with it. I did everything that I could to tear him down. That destructive behavior that I had

THE FINAL STRAW

developed early on still lived in me.

I let fear take over and because I was afraid of being hurt again, I became controlling beyond measure. I needed to be in control to make sure that the relationship went the way that I wanted it to. In reality what I was doing was tearing down this man's ego and driving him precisely in the opposite direction of where I wanted him to come. My mental instability made it very hard for him to love me.

I analyzed everything that he did. I would calculate the time that he got off of work added to the number of stop lights that he had to pass multiplied by the length of time that each light held and figure out the exact time he should have been walking through the front door. Of course there would be a million and one questions to answer if he wasn't there on time.

I was also good at analyzing his telephone voice to figure out if it was a male or female on the other end. First of all, let me mention this, his cell phone bet not ring and he don't answer it or push the little silence button. Oh, that was a fight right there. That was one of the worse things that he could do because now in my mind you're hiding something. Best to pick it up and tell the bitch you can't talk right now. It would be much better for you to answer and let a woman be on the other end than for you not to answer at all. This way, at least I'll know what I'm up against. I figured out that short responses meant that there was a woman on the phone. If the person on the other end would talk and then it's his turn and all he said was "yeah" and then dead silence then something wasn't right. No elaboration, no emphasis on the conversation! If the other person would say something else and if all I heard was "Uh huh" and then dead silence again, I knew then that there was a dam woman on the other end. I wasn't crazy. (At least that's my claim to fame). All that short talk meant "I can't talk right now."

Our battles also included a few physical altercations (usually provoked by me) where the police were called. I got so mad one night because it was 3oclock in the morning and he wasn't home. The rage that ran through me was too much for me to just lie there and wait for him to come home to fight. The only thing close enough to him that I could get my hands on to hurt him were his clothes. I grabbed every piece of clothing that he had in my house (which was a lot) and took and poured bleach on everything. Bro had some nice thick jeans and shirts. When I finished I dumped every stitch of it in a big Mapco gas station dumpster behind the store.

But when anger consumed me so much until I went to another woman's job that he had on the other end of the phone claiming that they were just "friends" discussing the basketball game that was on, I knew that I had lost all remaining self control. I made it to the burger joint and got out of the car. They actually were closed so I ended up banging on the door and cursing through the window like a mad woman. "I came up here to see who Justin is talking to on the phone. Yall don't know, I'll kill that MF. You better tell yo boy to stop messing with me", I shouted from the other side of the glass. The employees inside were looking like who the hell is that. After I had cursed the glass long enough and upon my departure I was so angry that I saw nothing but destruction. I put his car that I was driving in reverse and slammed it into the lady's car. In my defense though, because of my anger I didn't see that car. For real! She ran out and checked and as we looked we saw no damage. It was by the grace of God that they all didn't run out of that place and jump me claiming self-defense.

I was filled with rage and at the drop of a dime was ready to bust all the windows out of his car. I fantasized about that crowbar piercing the front windshield of that Lexus that *he* drove. That would hurt him more than anything else that I could have done to him. Men love their cars.

I was seriously out of control and at that point I realized that I needed help. I had lost it. I ran crying to that same aunt that wanted me when I was but a baby and from her house she called a crisis van that came and took me to Lakeside Hospital.

Upon arrival and after check-in the first thing that they did was took my shoestrings. There is nothing more degrading and humbling at the same time than having to surrender the very shoestrings out of your shoes. When they took them, I just knew that I wasn't coming out of that place. My first night in the 'joint', I cried like a baby. I looked around and saw all kinds of women. There were young women, old women, black women, white women, poor women, rich women. It was a very sad scene.

By the next morning, I pretended to be all right though. I couldn't cry anymore and decided to act sane so that I could get out quicker. I quickly assumed my position as kind of the leader in the joint. I didn't do this on purpose. My chipper "good morning everyone", made the ladies feel that I had something that they didn't have. What that could have been I didn't know. I was in the same medicine line that they were in twice a day. As I listened to their stories, I seemed to be able to say something to them that made them feel better. As we sat on the barred and screened in porch, the only piece of outside that we could get to, I would sing to them. Now I'm not prejudice at all but it was kind of funny to hear white women shouting Hallelujah. It was like we were at church right there on that back porch in the mental institution. When they were feeling down, they would ask me to sing to them and I would. One girl found leisure in braiding my hair; another one gave me her favorite pair of pajamas, (yes I still have them); another girl gave me her Bible that was very special to her, (and yes I still have it too). One lady in there was very rich. She would always ask me if I wanted her to get some money for me. "No", I told her. "I'm all right in here. I don't plan to be here long." It seemed that I had something inspirational to say to them all and it wasn't long before I had them all up dancing around the lounge area. I taught them my favorite thing to do of course, that electric slide. It was hilarious to see women with no rhythm try to keep up when it was time to turn. But they were having fun. The nurses shouted to me from their nursing station "Mrs. Davis, we're going to have to keep you in here." I stopped in my tracks and looked at them as I thought, "the devil is a lie."

While my visit to Lakeside Mental Behavioral Facility was filled with rest and peace I knew that I had to get my mind thinking right so

WHAT WAS MEANT FOR MY BAD...

that I would not have to come back. In order for me to do that I realized that I had to let some things go. I had to cut relational ties with people and things that would cause me to spend out of control again. I had to let go of all ungodly relationships; romantic and otherwise. I even had to cut ties with my family so that I could heal. Yeah I wanted to love everybody but I knew that I was going to get nowhere but trips to Lakeside trying to build relationships with people who had not learned how to love. "Except the Lord build a house, they labour in vain that build it" (Psalm 127:1). I had to step off and learn to love myself. Then came a mighty and wonderful change to my life.

-16-

Restoration

AS YOU HAVE read, my life certainly has not been without devastation. It is that same devastation, however, that has grown me into the pillar of strength that I am today; able to stand and help heal others.

Because my childhood was filled with sexual abuse, I stand well qualified to mentor today's young children who has experienced the same. Such mentorship is vital in helping them to heal and understand that what happened wasn't their fault.

Since I escaped the hand of domestic violence, I am greatly suited to convince young ladies that he is indeed **not** "beating you because he loves you". I know now that you don't hurt what you love. A man that beats a woman has his own internal issues that need to be addressed; and please know that if he hits you once, he will hit you again. Very rarely without intervention does the situation gets better; it only gets worse. Because my life has been filled with promiscuity, I can lend a hand with talking to those who walk our streets selling their bodies, not knowing that they have a greater value. While I know how an individual can come to feel like that is all they are worth, I also know that through the renewing of the mind, that feeling can be dispelled.

I can testify that perhaps sometimes your mental state can not handle all that burdens it at a given time. We may sometimes give way to mental instability, but even that can be stabilized with a good support system in place. That support system may be in the form of professional doctors, spiritual leaders, or maybe just someone you've come to trust and can confide in. I've learned that talking it out can be a cure for a lot of issues that we face.

Out of all the experiences that I have to share with others, the greatest one of all came when I made ONE conscious decision that changed my life forever. I decided to LOVE MYSELF. Whether anyone else loved me or not. I purposely and selfishly put me first in my own life. I decided to learn me and discover who I truly am. After that, I vowed to work on the things that would make me even better.

I took advantage of programs that were offered to help with the quality of life for myself and my children. I set goals and developed a plan of action to achieve them. I started to look at where I wanted to be six months from now, one year from now, etc. I used a journal to track my progress.

I even jotted down the characteristics I wanted in a mate. I would tolerate no more abuse. I had to let go of what I was taught by Killa, Ray Ray, Frederick, Mo Money...the rest. I started learning new characteristics from men who treated their wives in a manner that made my soul long to be treated the same way. I will no longer lower my standards to be with someone, rather they will have to raise their standards to be with me.

I have become a far better mother than I imagined that I ever could be. I laugh when I tell my children today that I definitely want a Mother's Day gift on Mother's Day. I have actually earned that "right". I never thought that I would be at ballet rehearsals nor basketball practices; but I am. Sometimes stretched out sleep in the car outside the dance studio, but I'm there. I never thought that I would have children that would be so smart that the schools actually rely on them on major testing days to bring up the overall score of the entire school; but I do. All four of them.

The bottom line, like Whitney Houston said "The greatest love of all is easy to achieve. Learning to love yourself. It is the greatest love of all." So I truly do love me and have learned to embrace every aspect of my life. I find myself starring in the mirror and telling my reflection how awesome I really am. To have come through so much and still stand. To be able and willing to write about it to help you stand too.

I want to encourage each of you to do likewise. Learn to love yourself! It's okay. Soul search and find out who you really are without any concerns about who others *say* that you are. Work on the areas in your life that you need to make better. Live the best you that you can possibly live. Afterall, can't nobody do you like you can do you.

Use my testimony as a reference if you forget that you are worthy to be loved.

It is my desire now to travel the country to meet God's people and share my new spirit and message of love in person to all that will embrace it. To the abused, neglected, and the forgotten. To those with stories like mine. I would love to take a stand and be the advocate against the phrase 'Shhh, don't tell nobody". So let me start by leaving you with this new life changing phrase, "talk and tell somebody and somebody else if you must".

And remember, What Was Meant For Your Bad Just Might Make You Better!

Be blessed!

I would like to give a special thanks to Elizabeth K. Cross.
I would like to send a shout out to F. Martin and J. Swan.

CPSIA information can be obtained
at www.ICGtesting.com
Printed in the USA
JSHW020252071221
20997JS00002B/20

9 781478 750710